SRA

Reading Mastery

Signature Edition

Language Arts Answer Key

Grade 1

Siegfried Engelmann
Jean Osborn
Karen Lou Seitz Davis

McGraw Hill SRA

Columbus, OH

SRAonline.com

McGraw Hill SRA

Printed in the United States of America.

Send all inquiries to this address:
SRA/McGraw-Hill
8787 Orion Place
Columbus, OH 43240-4027

ISBN: 978-0-07-612488-6
MHID: 0-07-612488-6

6 7 8 9 10 11 12 13 GLO 16 15 14 13 12

The McGraw·Hill Companies

Name ______________________________

1

Purple plums, porch floor, and top of window.
P
P
P
P

1

R
R
R
R
Y
Y
Y
Y

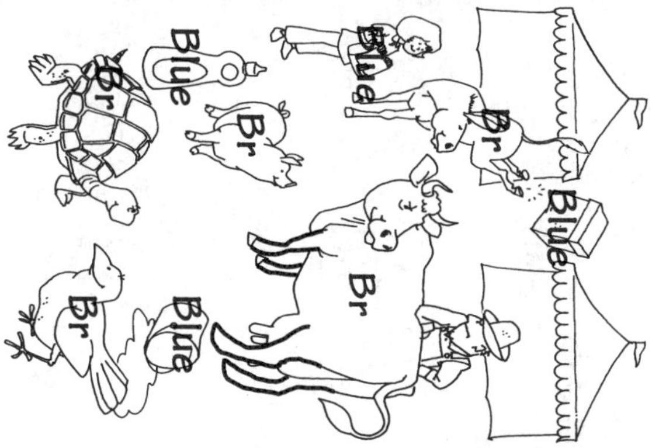

Blue
Blue
Blue
Blue
Br
Br
Br
Br
Br

Name ______________________________

2

Green fish.
Yellow fish.

2

Cats any color
Black
Black
Black
Black
G
G
G
G

Y
Y
Y
Y
B
B
B
B

Name ______________________________

3

Children color the birds various colors: red, yellow, brown, and spotted.

Lesson 3 Side 1

3

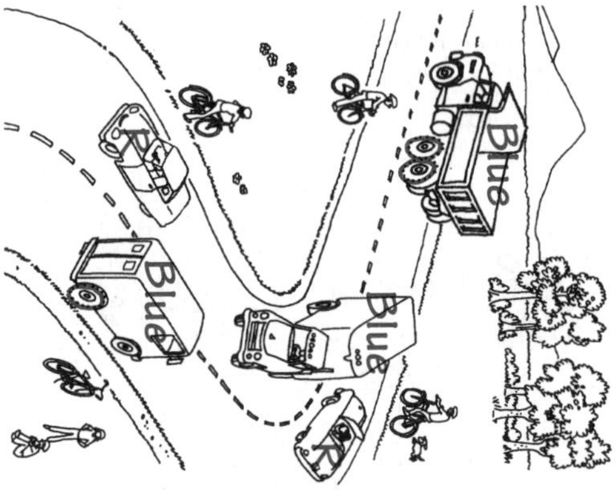

Side 2 Lesson 3

2

Name ______________________________

4

Purple plums, porch floor, whole window, smear on brother's pants, most of wall.

Lesson 4 Side 1

4

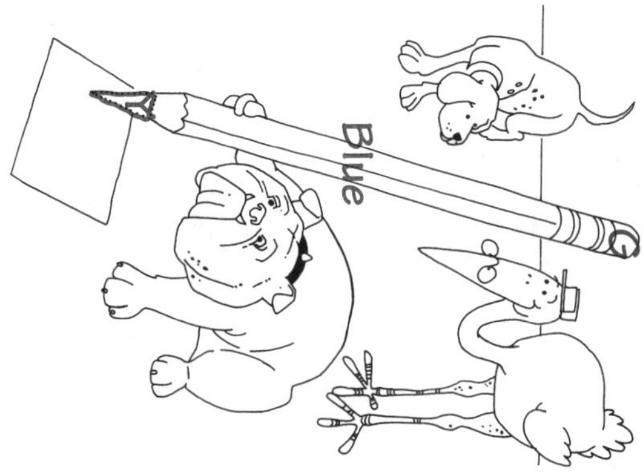

Side 2 Lesson 4

Name ______________________________ **5**

5

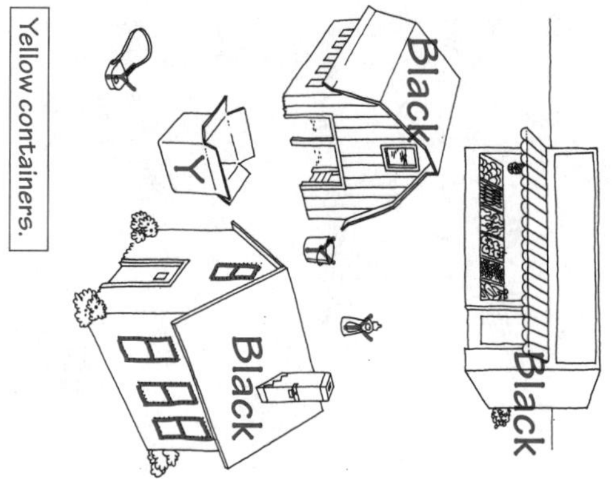

Name ______________________________ **6**

Name ______________________________ **7**

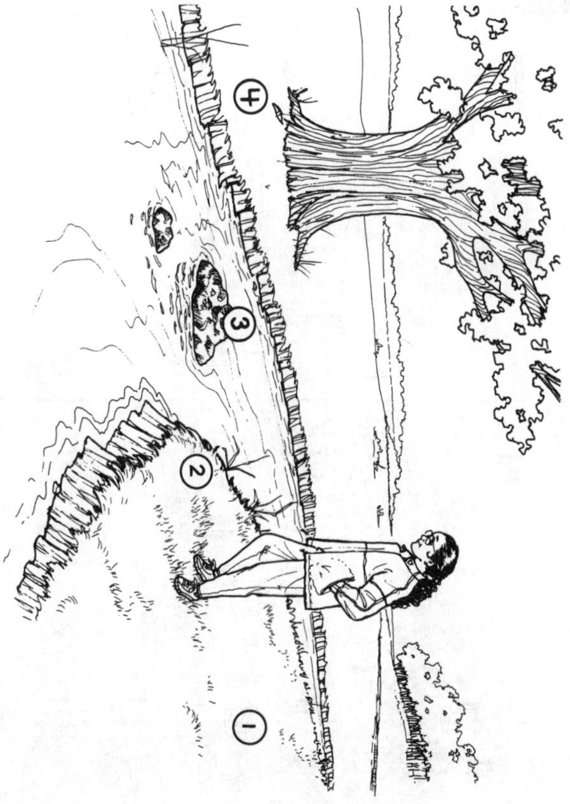

7

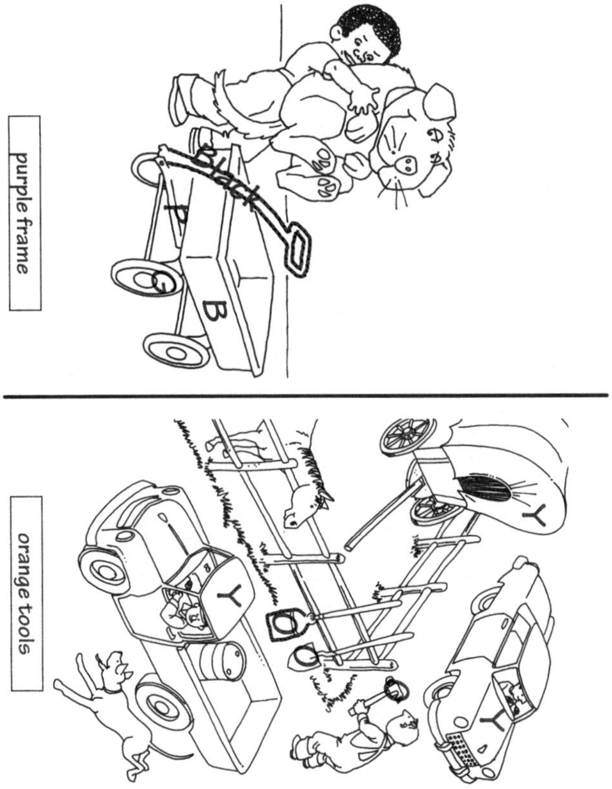
purple frame
Black
orange tools

Name ______________________

8

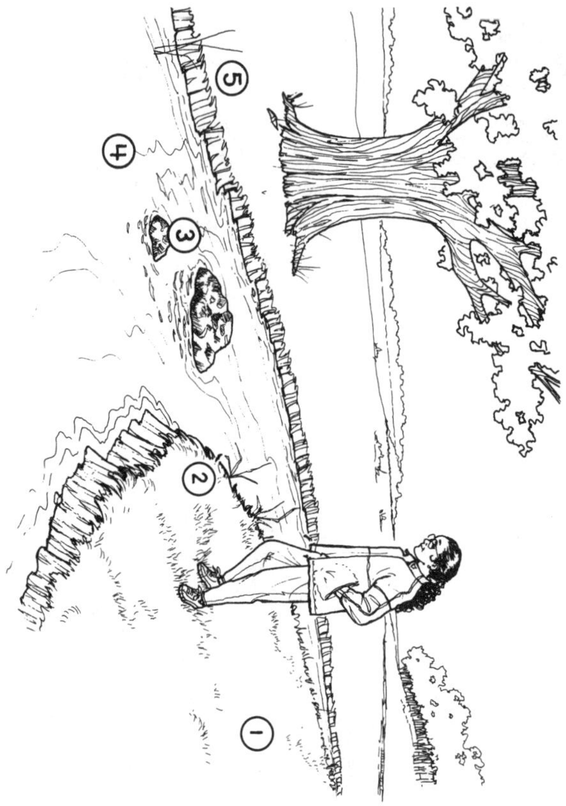

8

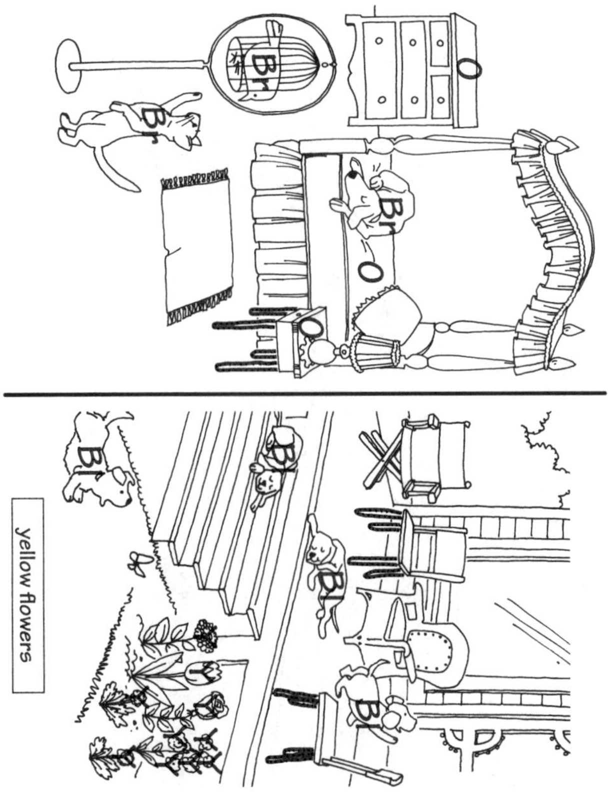
yellow flowers

Name ______________________

9

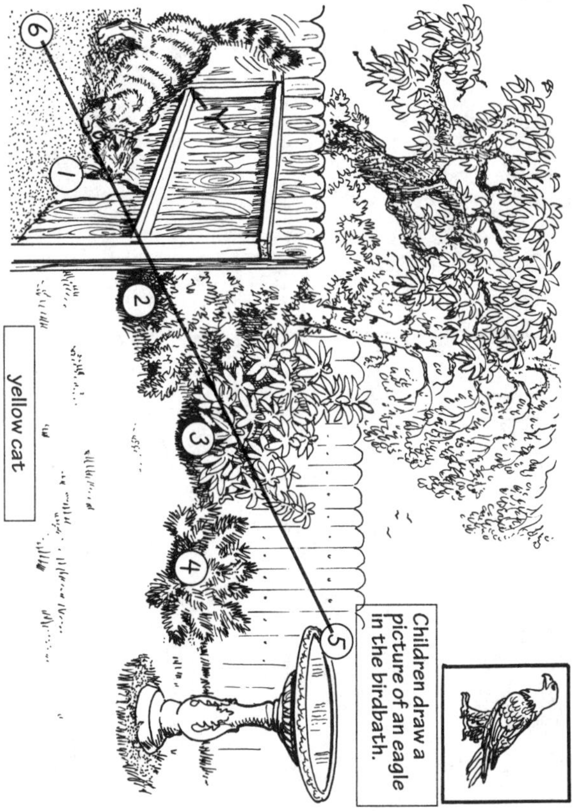
yellow cat
Children draw a picture of an eagle in the birdbath.

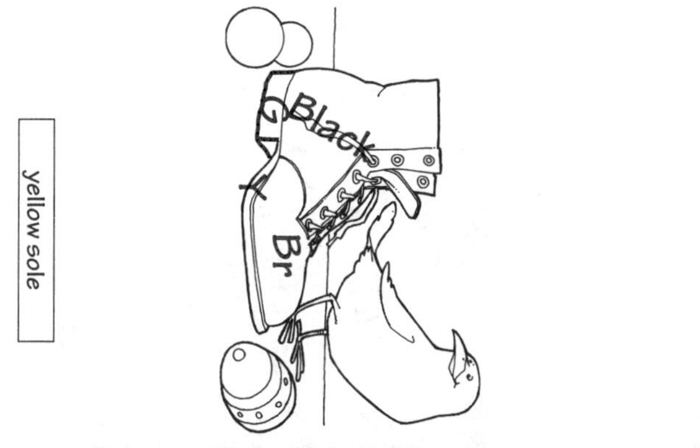

Name ______________________

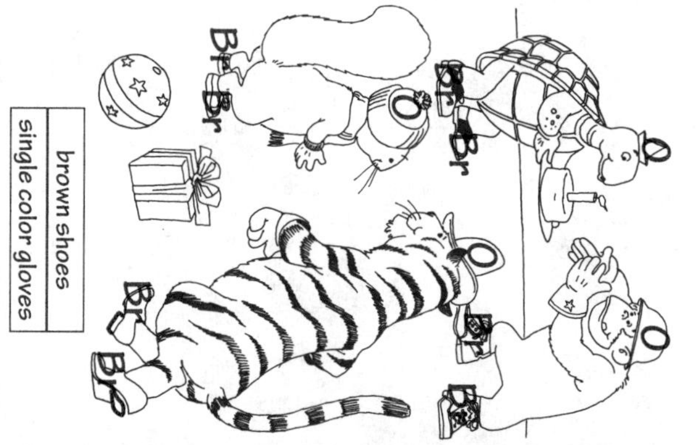
brown shoes
single color gloves

Children color some of the farm animals black and some of them brown.
R
R

Name ______________________

Optional: Child colors objects ①-④ pink.

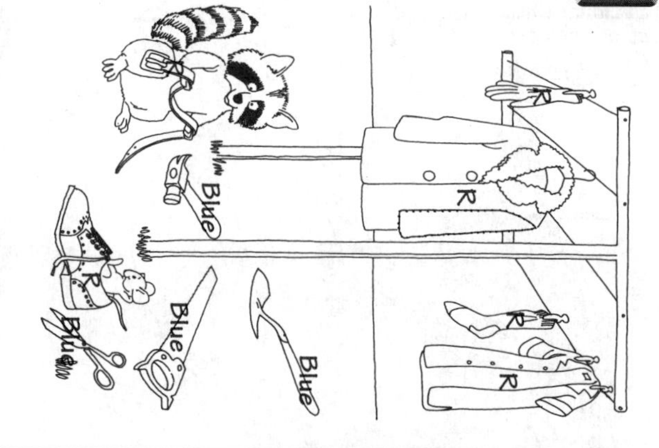

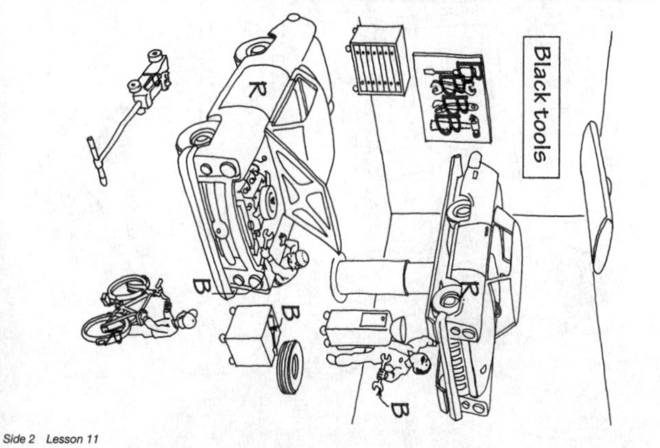
Black tools
R
R
B
B
B

Name ____________________

12

12

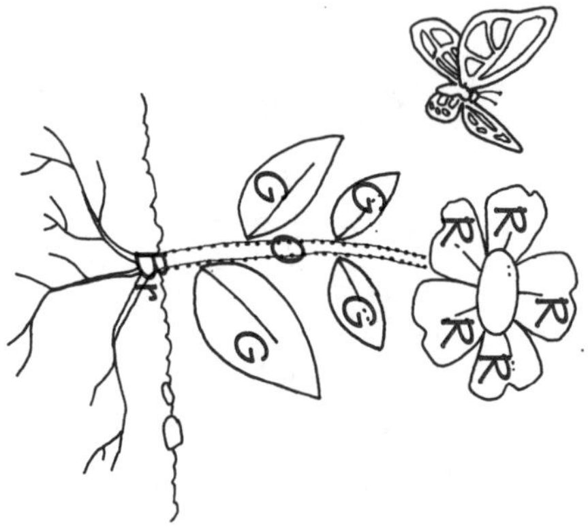

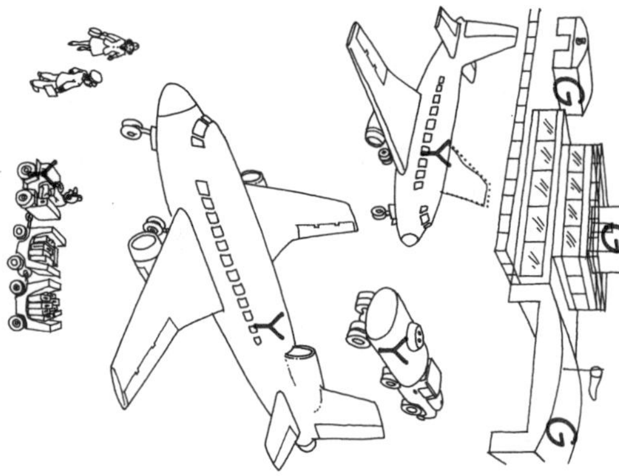

Name ____________________

13

13

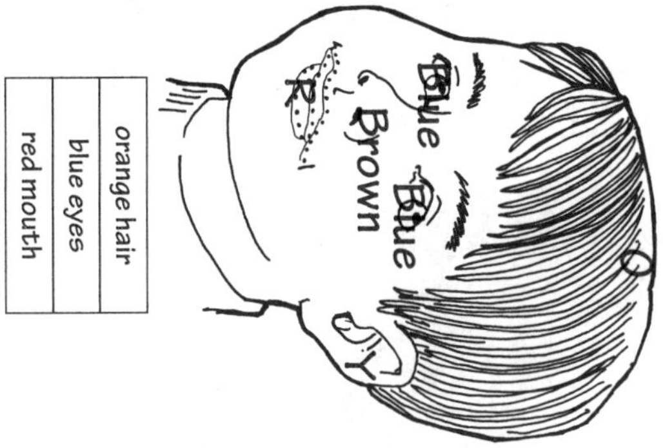

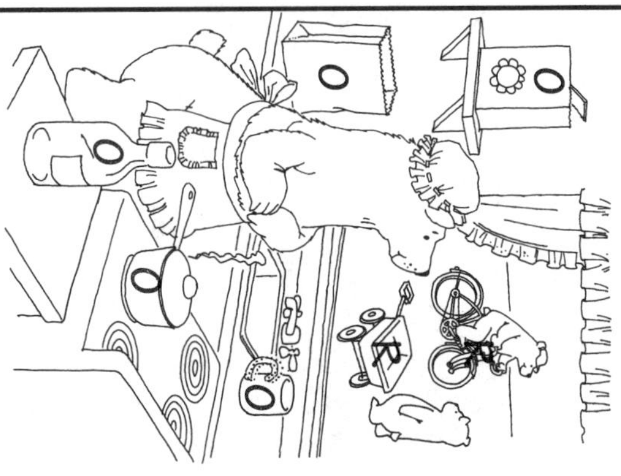

Name ______________________________

14

Lesson 14 Side 1

14

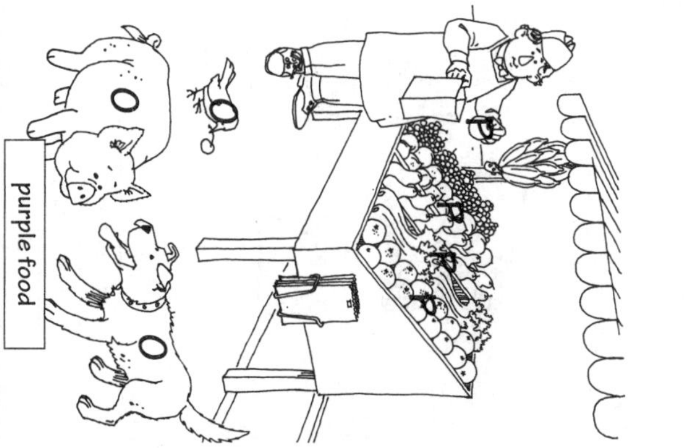

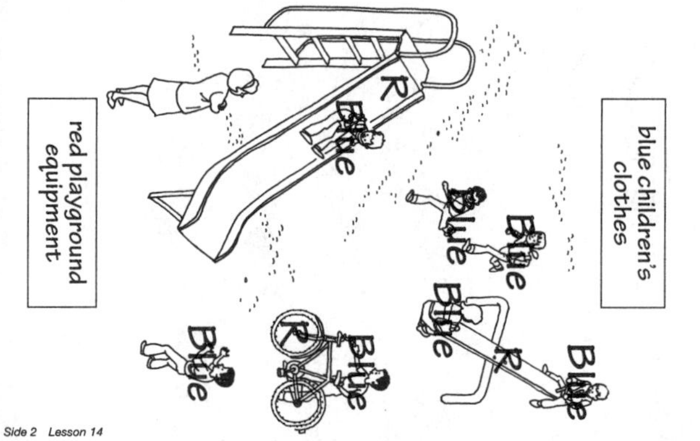

Side 2 Lesson 14

Name ______________________________

15

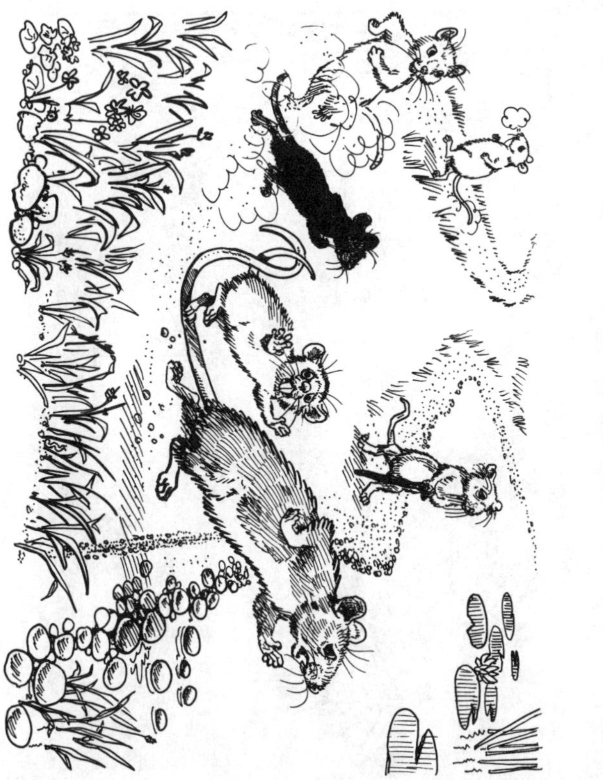

Lesson 15

Name ______________________________

16

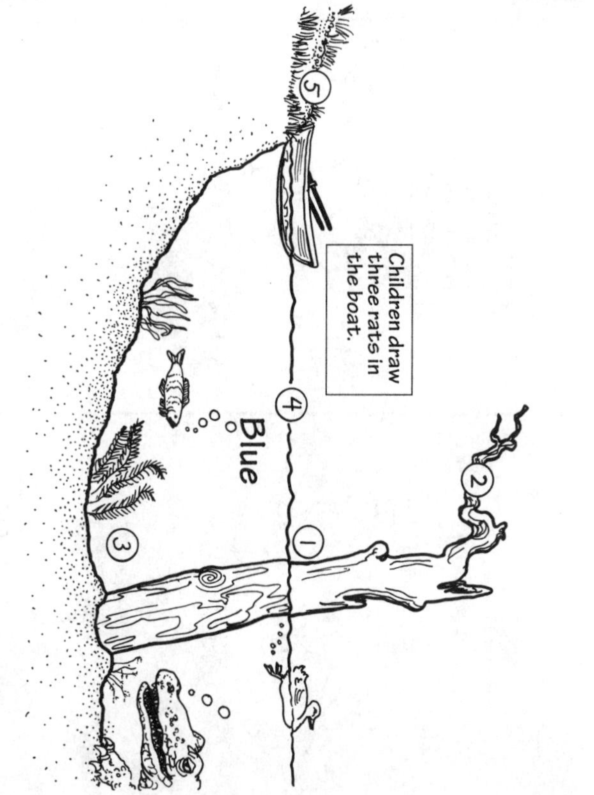

Lesson 16 Side 1

16

red chair rungs
green chair legs

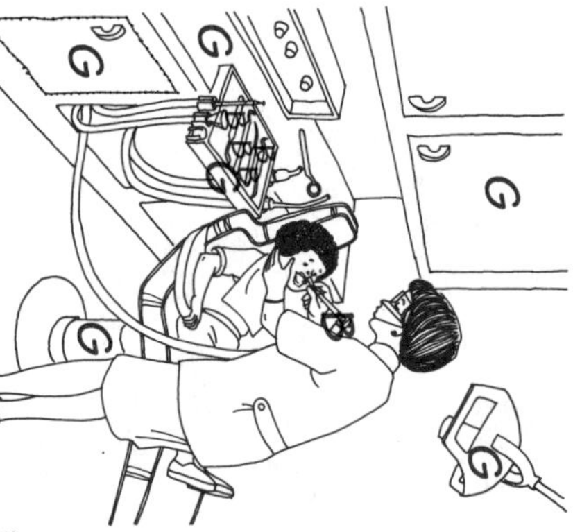

green furniture
blue tools

Name ______________________________

17

pink paddle, purse, plate

17

red roots, brown trunk and branches, green leaves

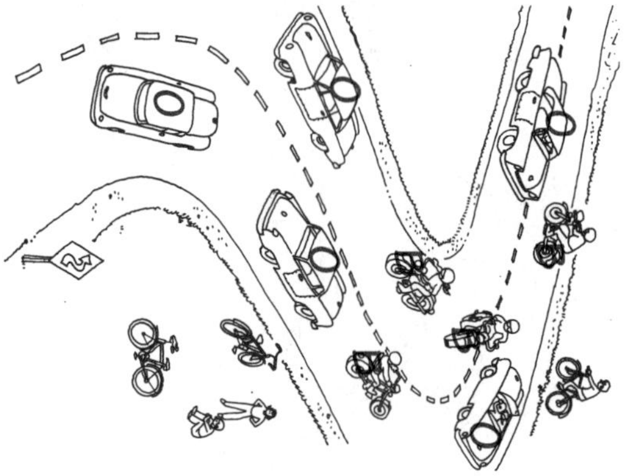

blue motorcycles

Name ______________________________

18

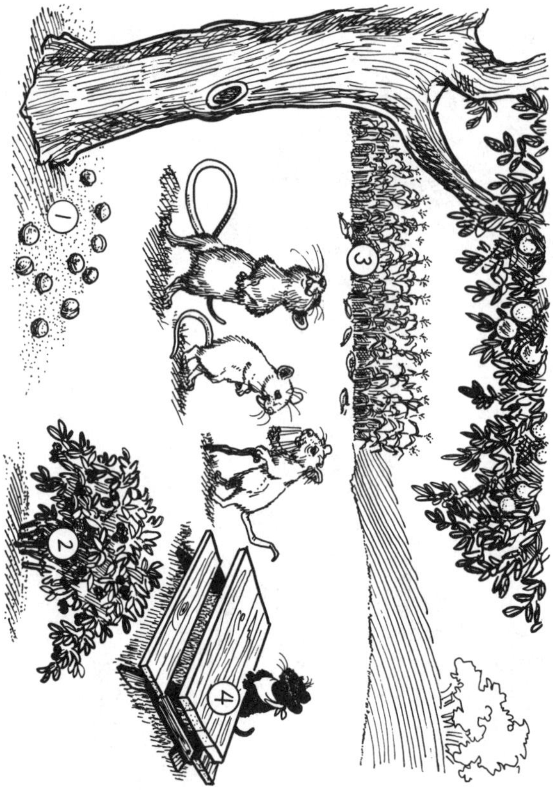

18

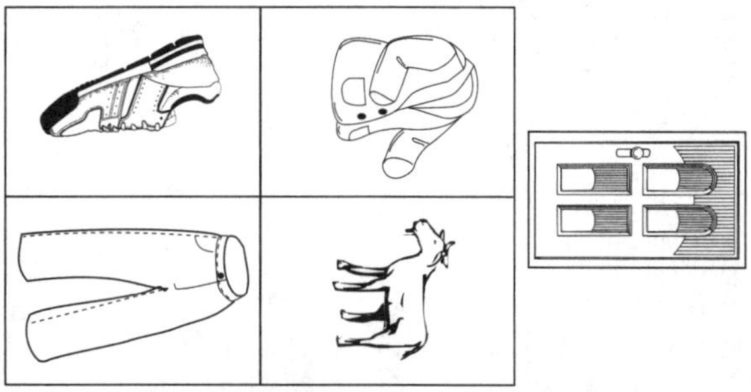

Name ______________________________

19

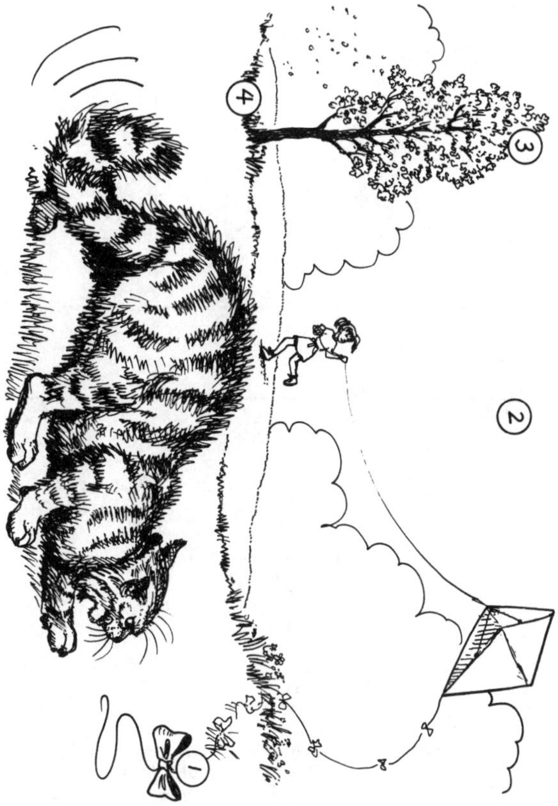

19

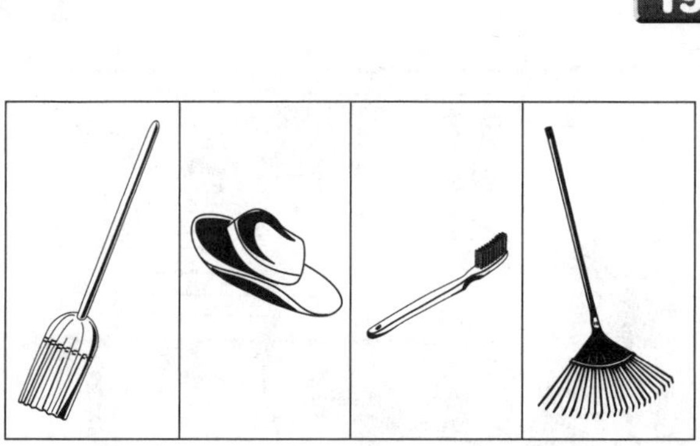

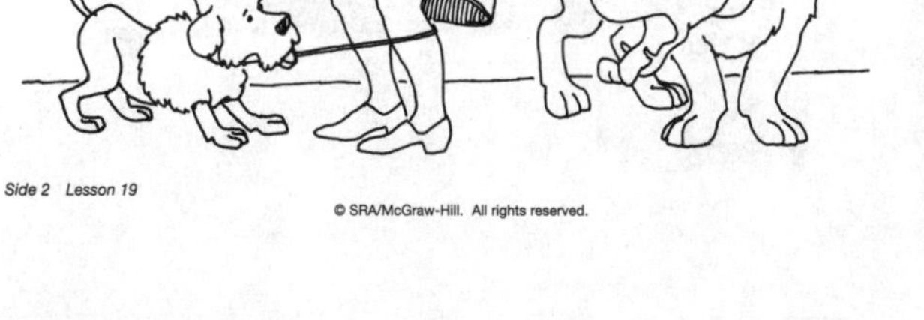

Name ______________________________

20

purple trunk,
black tail, brown
head, blue legs

Name _____

brown and white
cows, blue birds

Name _____

brown and white
cows, blue birds

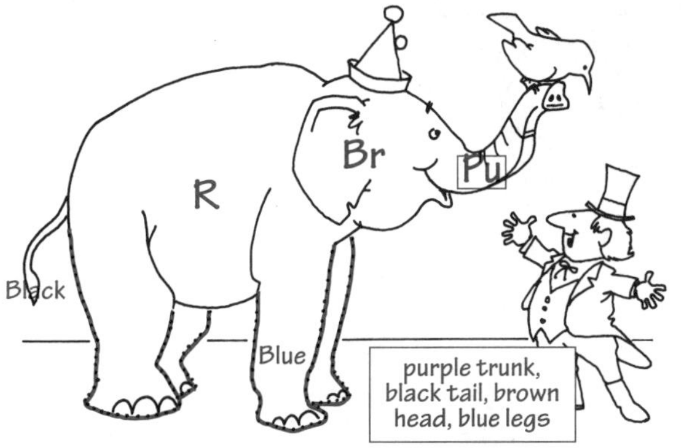

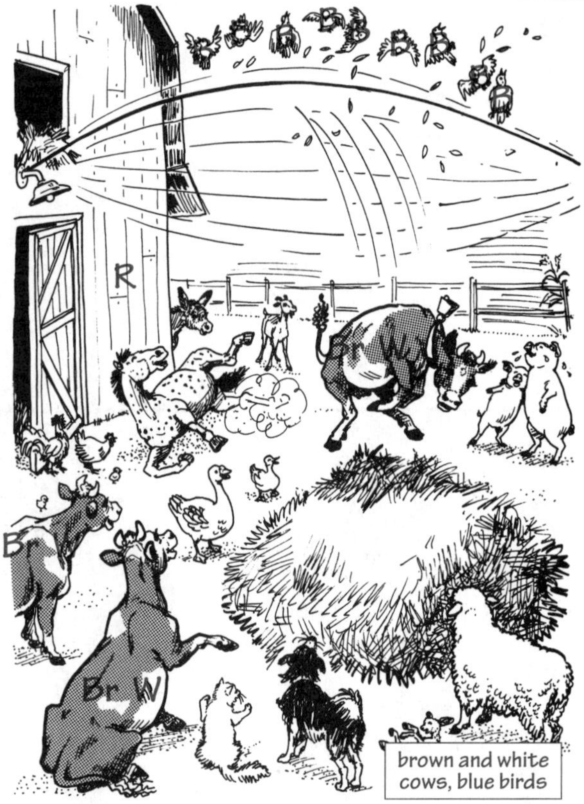

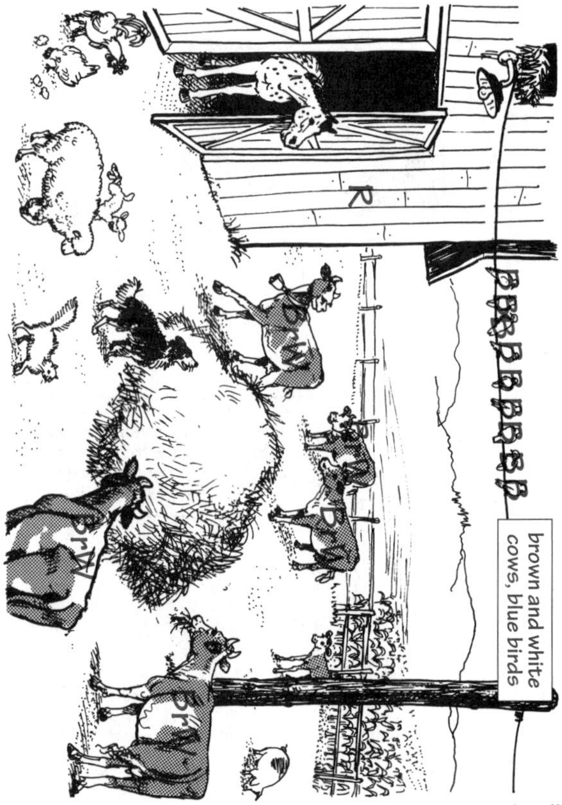

22

Name ________________________

23

23

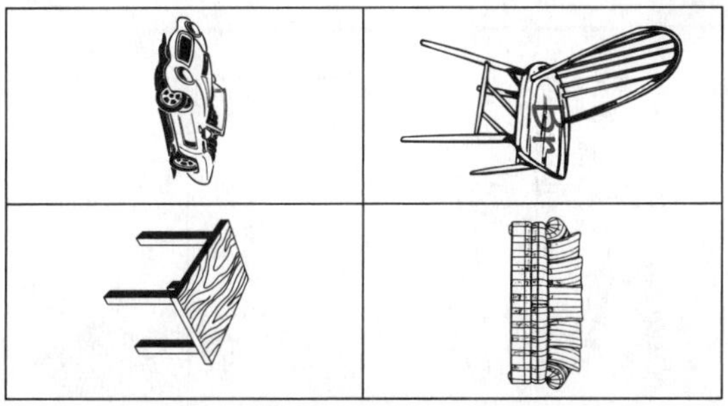

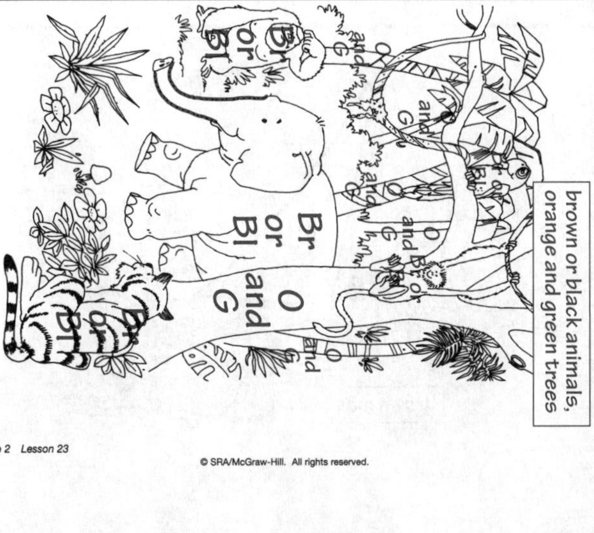

Name ________________________

24

Name ______________________________

25

25

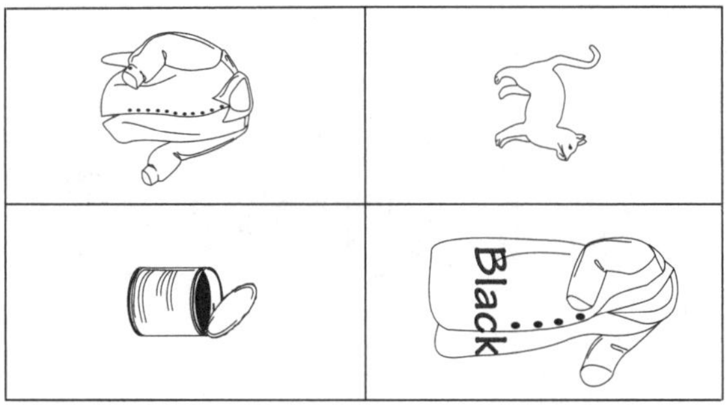

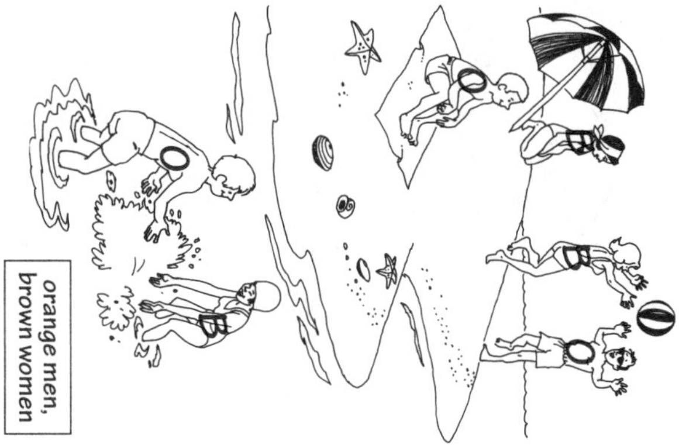

Name ______________________________

26

26

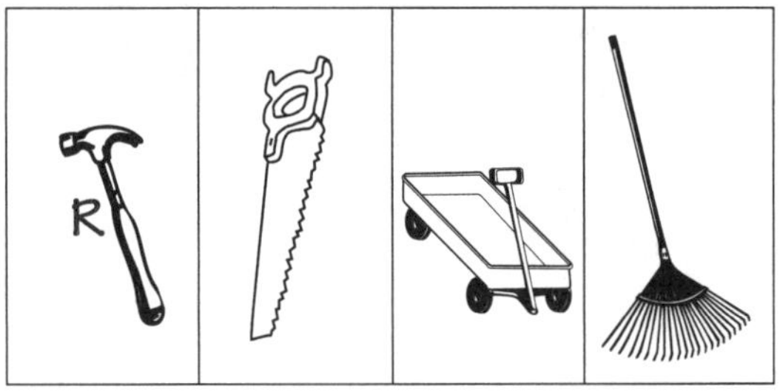

Name _____

27

Child writes numbers 2-4 in circles of choice and colors numbered items pink.

27

13

Name _____

28

brown and white dog, gray mouse

28

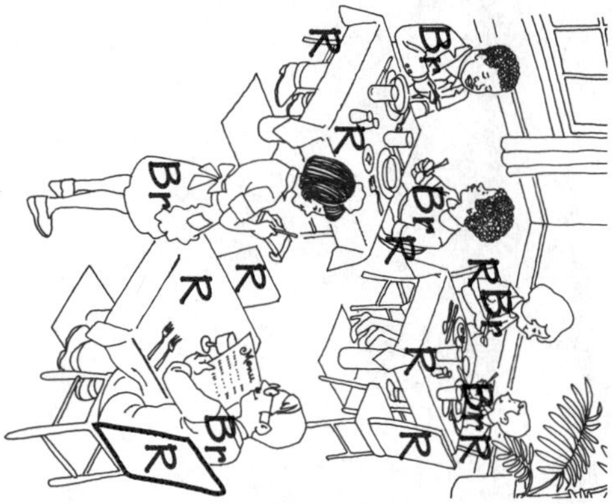

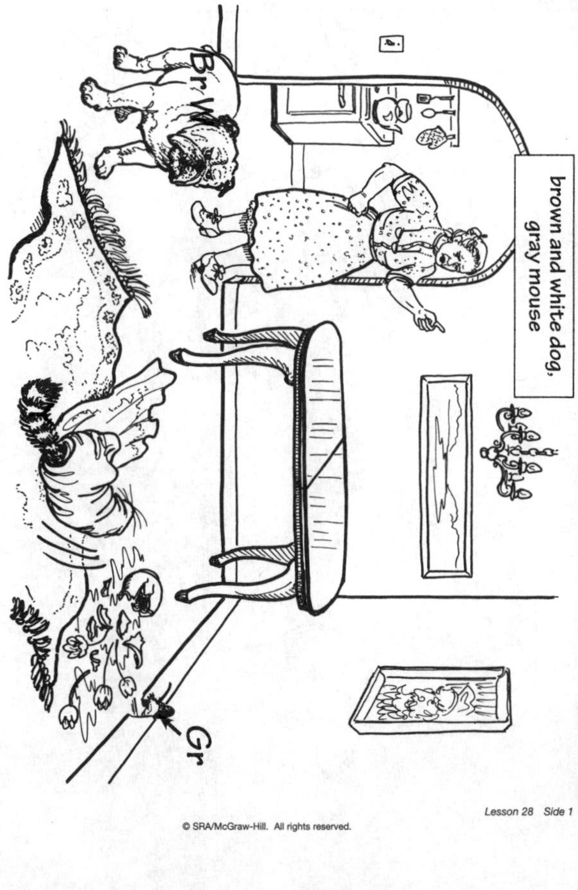

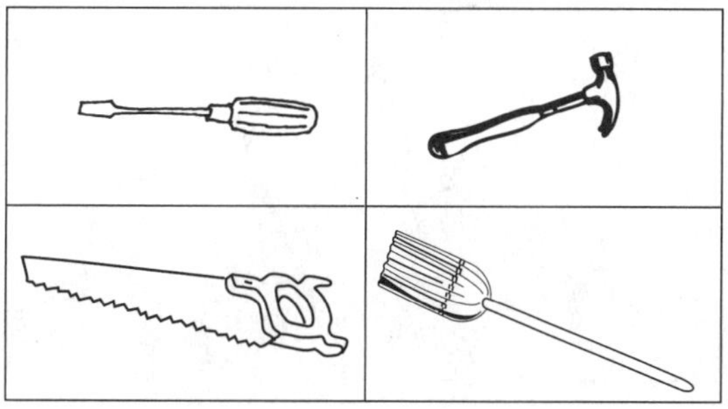

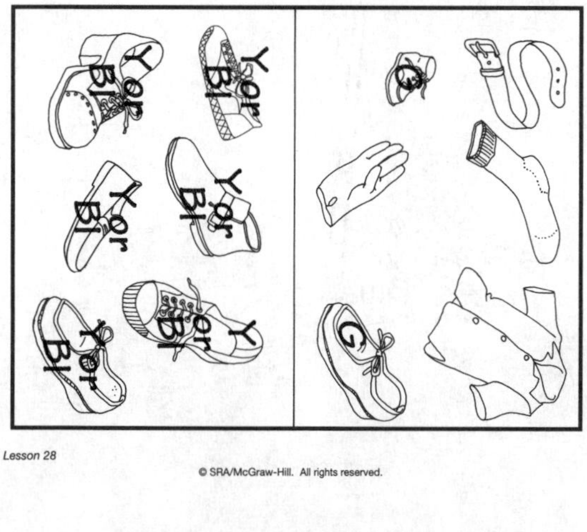

29

Lesson 29 Side 1

29

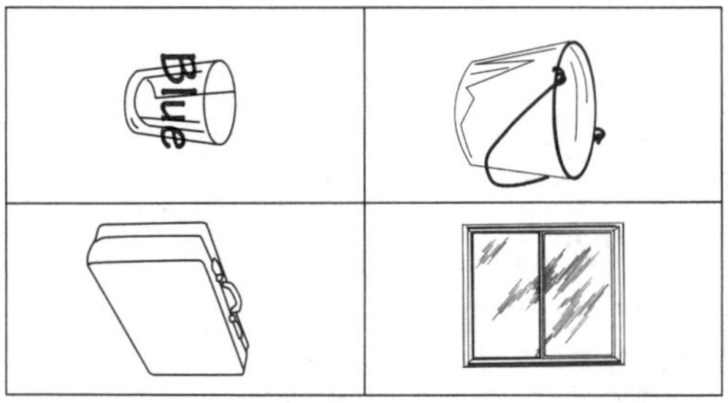

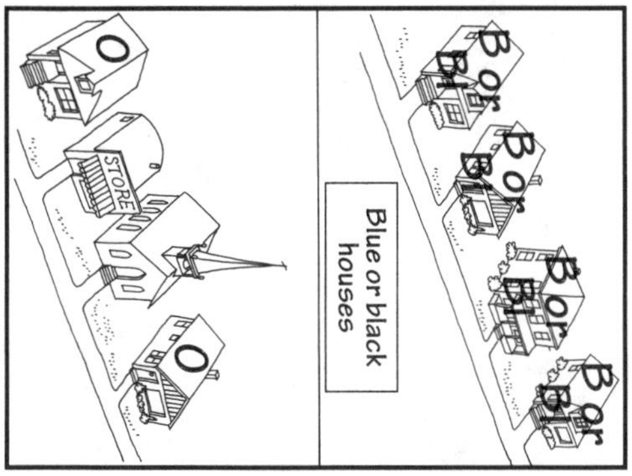

Side 2 Lesson 29

Name ______________________

30

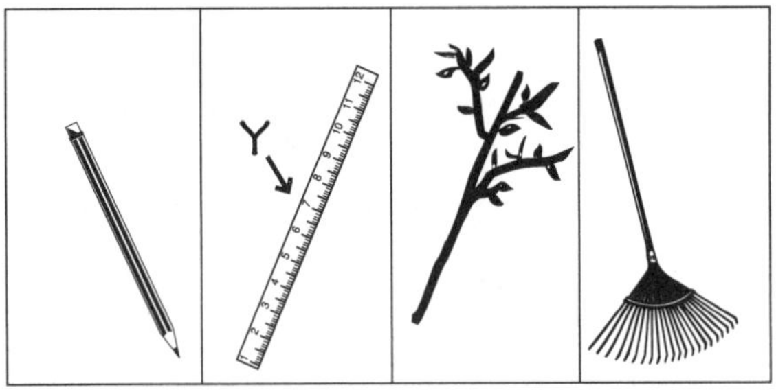

Lesson 30

Name ______________________

31

Lesson 31 Side 1

31

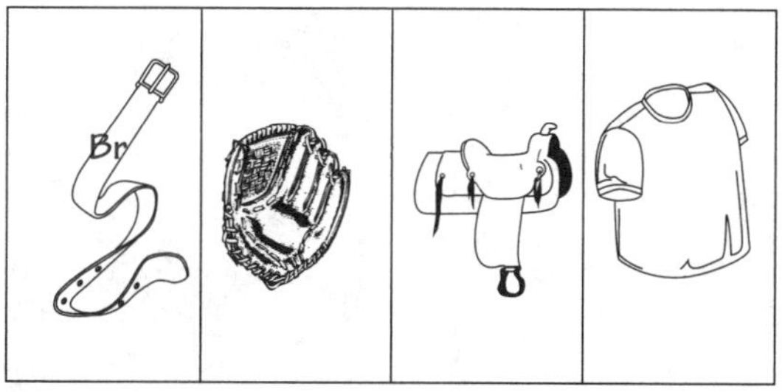

Name ______________________

32

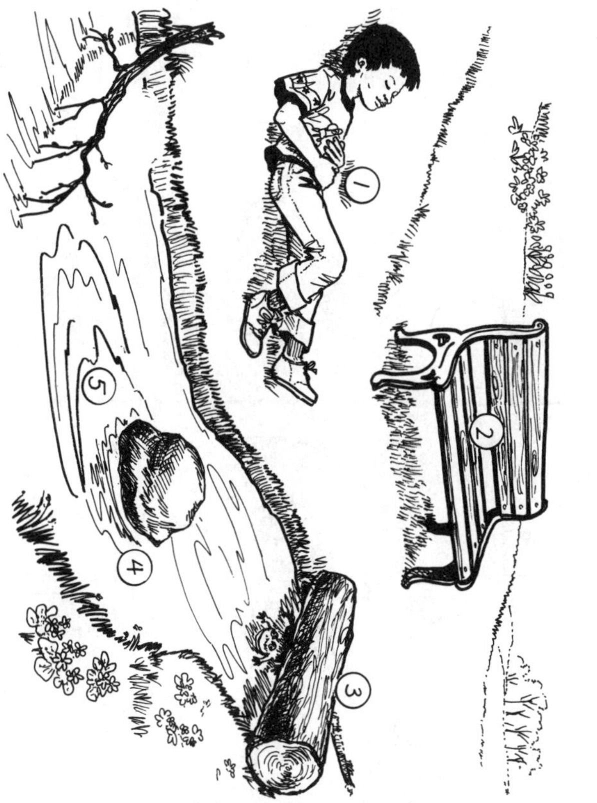

32

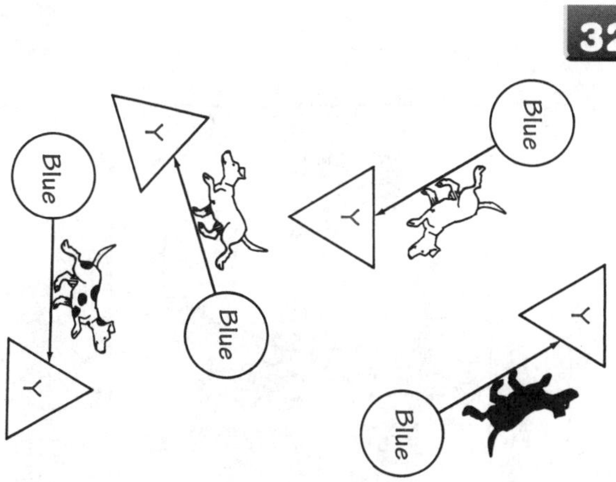

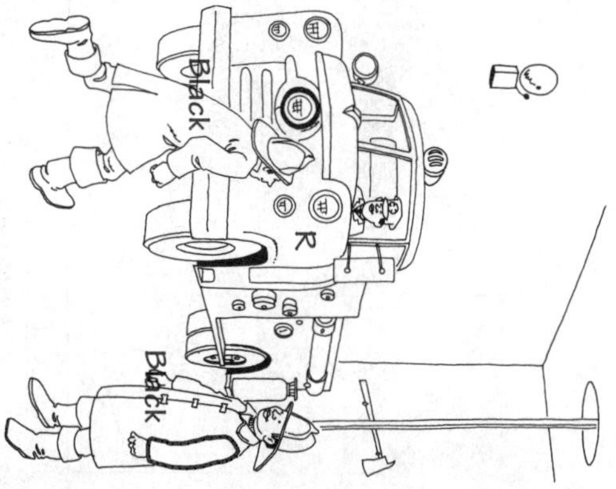

Name ______________________

33

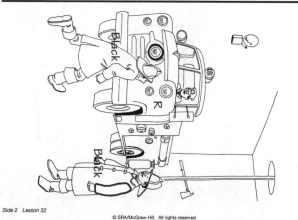

Child draws more rocks.

Name _____ 34

purple umbrella handle,
green covering

Lesson 34

Name _____ 35

Lesson 35   Side 1

16

35

Name _____ 36

blue birds

brown and white Clarabelle

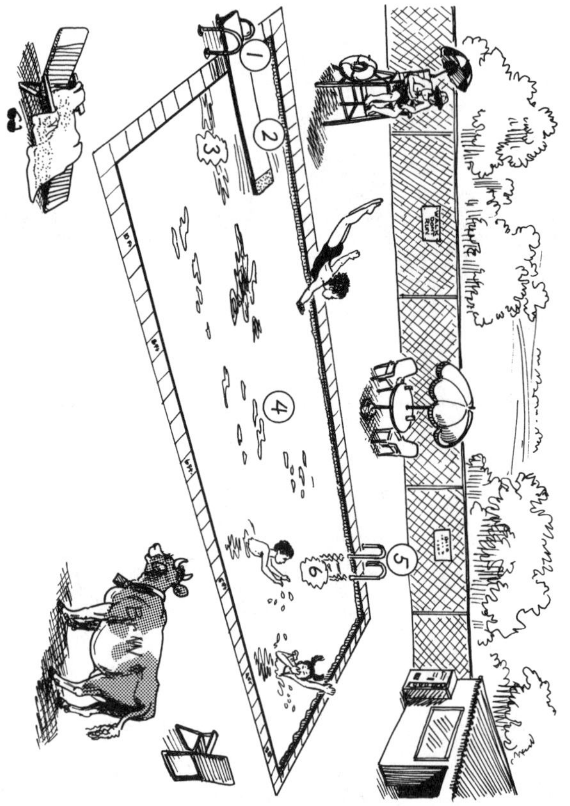

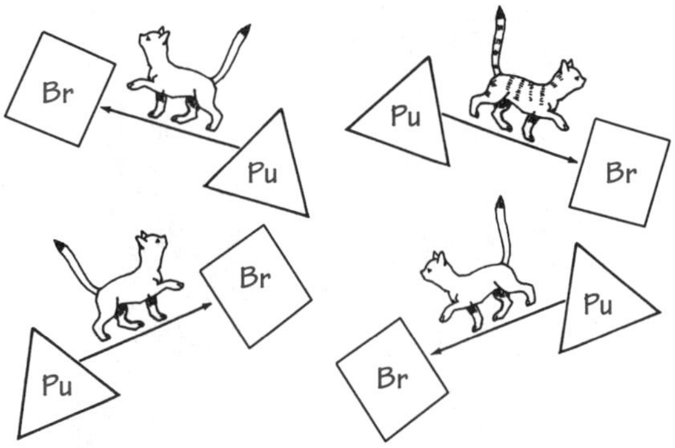

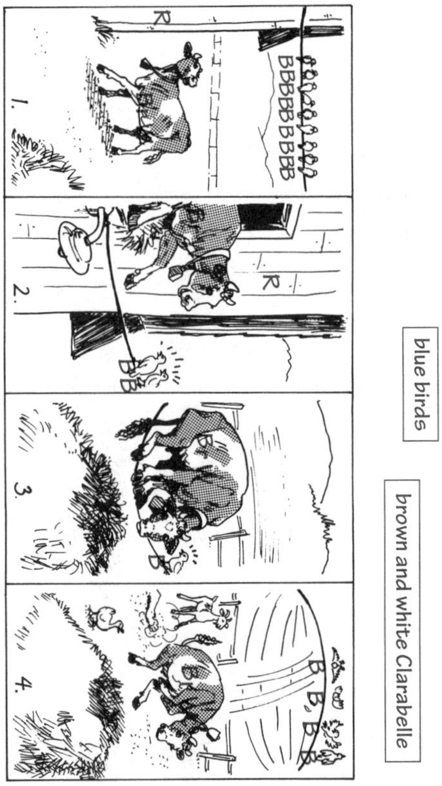

36

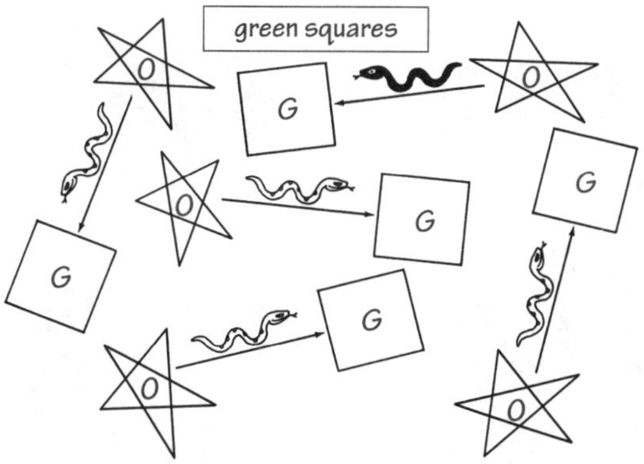
green squares
G
O

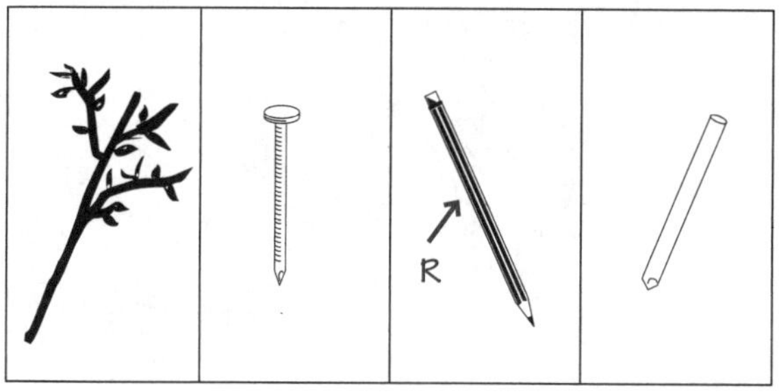

Name ______________________________

37

Optional: Child adds rocks.

Name ______________________________

38

childen color picture but
keep horse #7 white

38

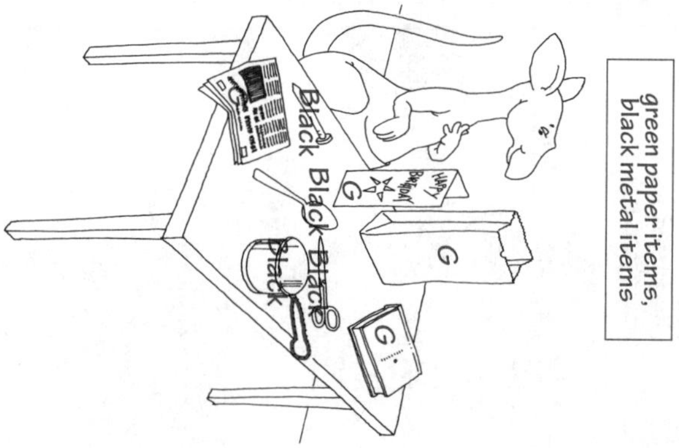
green paper items,
black metal items
Black
G

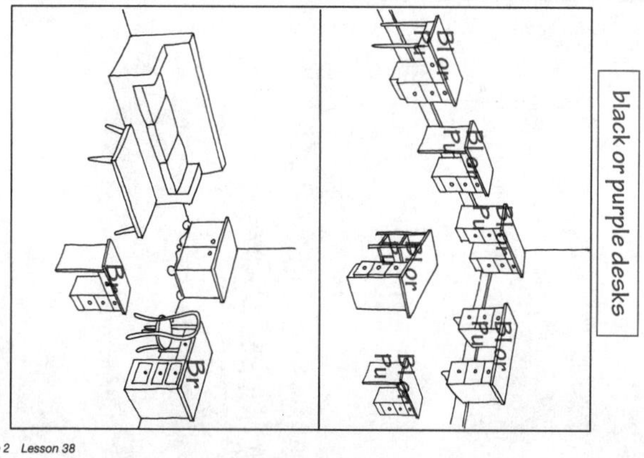

Name _____

yellow pencils

purple rubber items, yellow cloth items

18

Name _____

blue or purple dresses

green dresses

Black

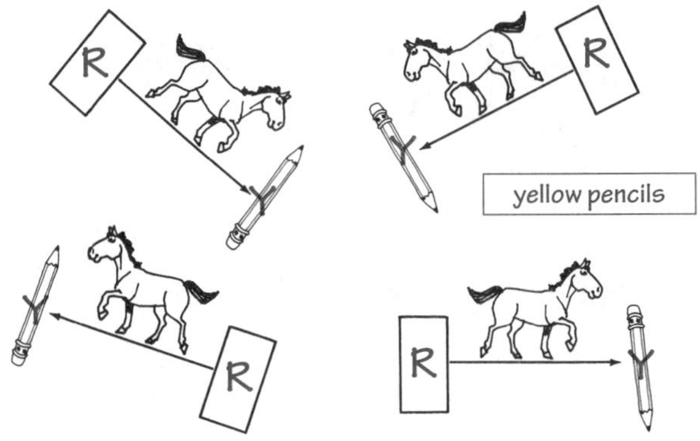

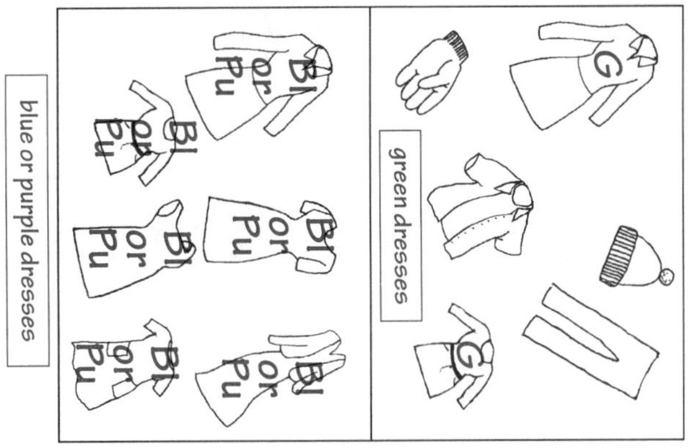

Name ______________________________

41

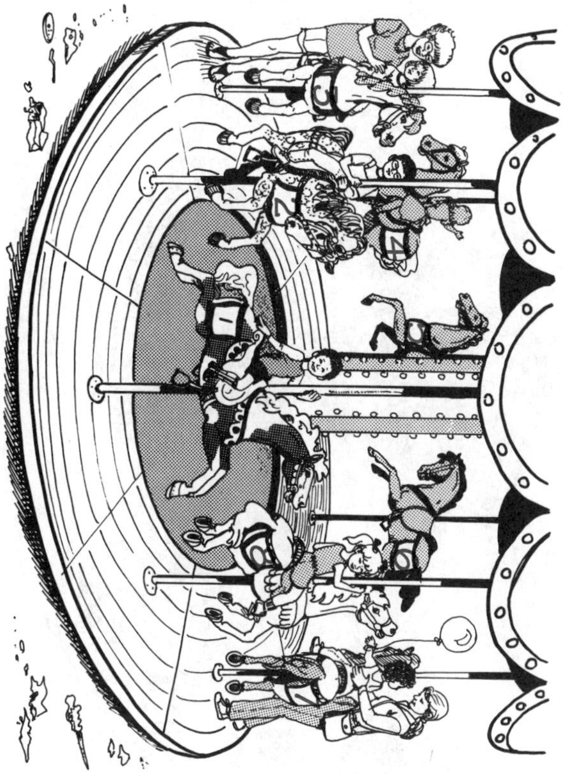

41

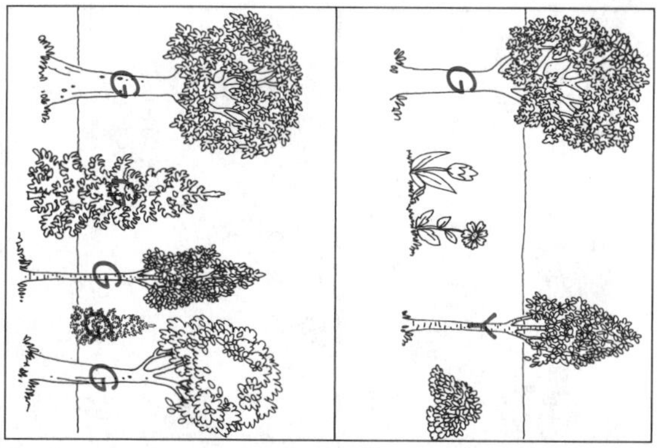

Name ______________________________

42

R	Red birds	10
Y	Yellow birds	6
B	Blue birds	7
	Other animals	2

Name ______________________________

43

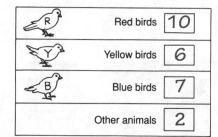

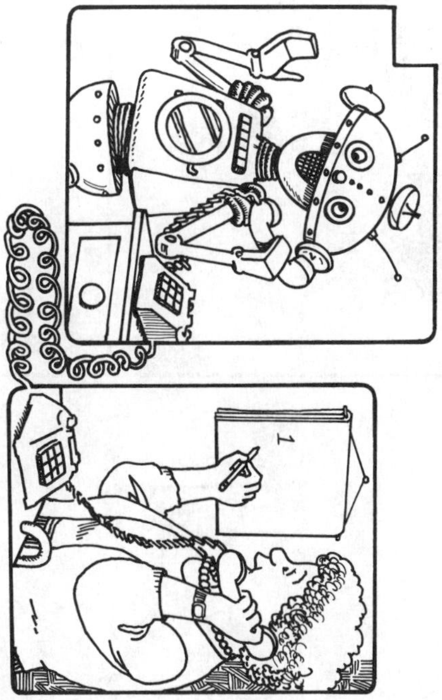

43

Name ______________________________

44

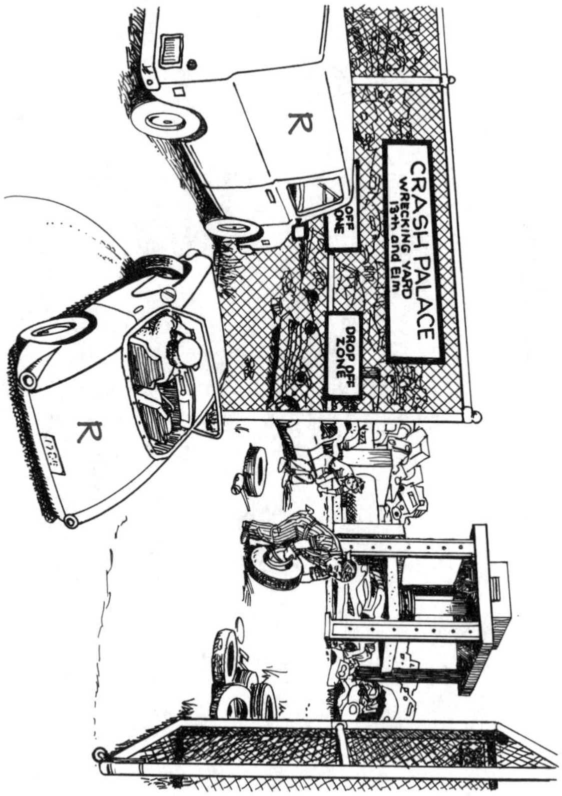

44

Name ______________________________

45

45

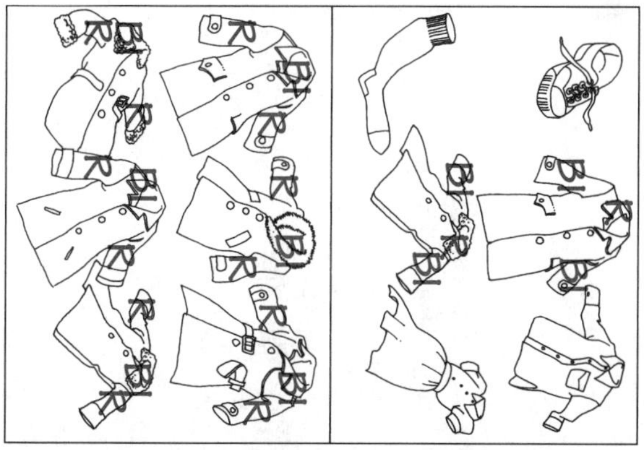

Name ______________________________

46

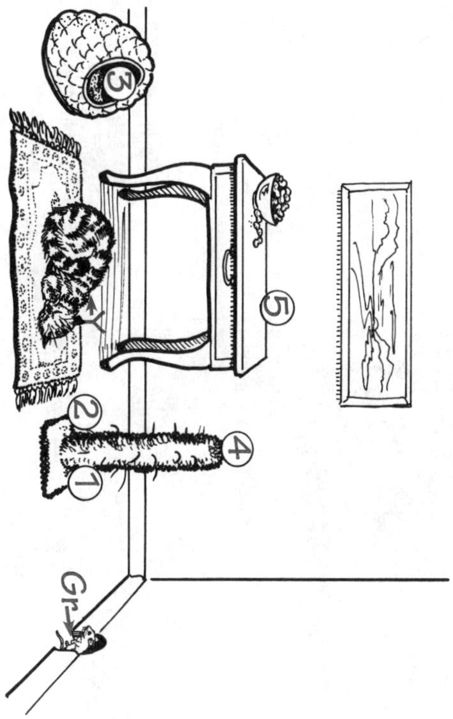

Name ______________________________

47

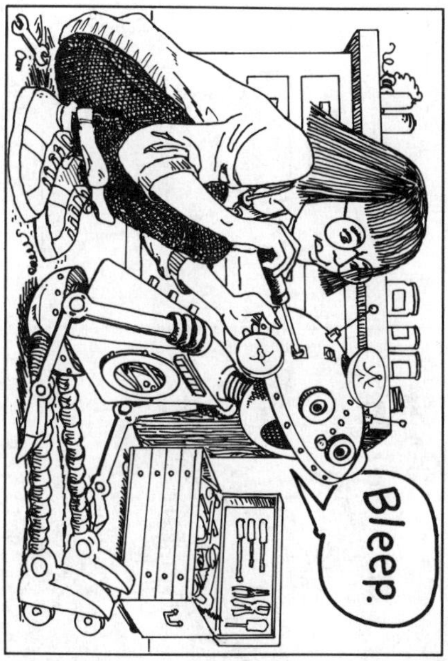

47

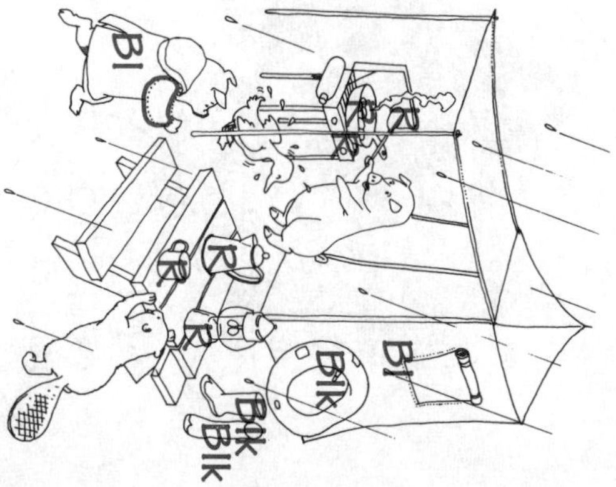

Name ______________________________

48

Lesson 48 Side 1

48

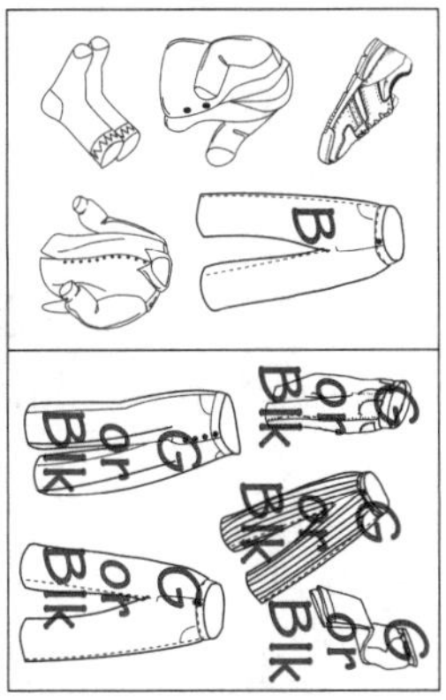

Side 2 Lesson 48

Name ______________________________

49

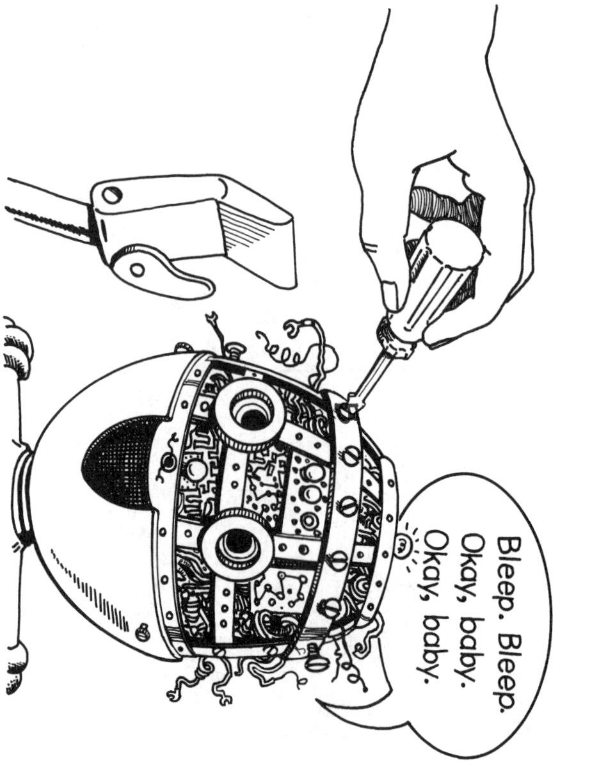

Lesson 49 Side 1

49

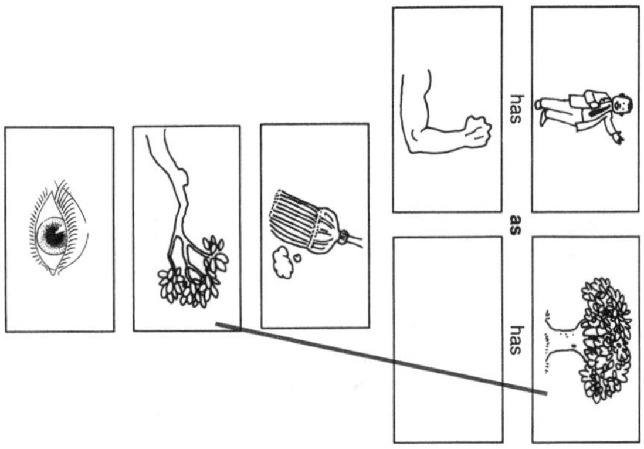

Side 2 Lesson 49

Name ______________________________

50

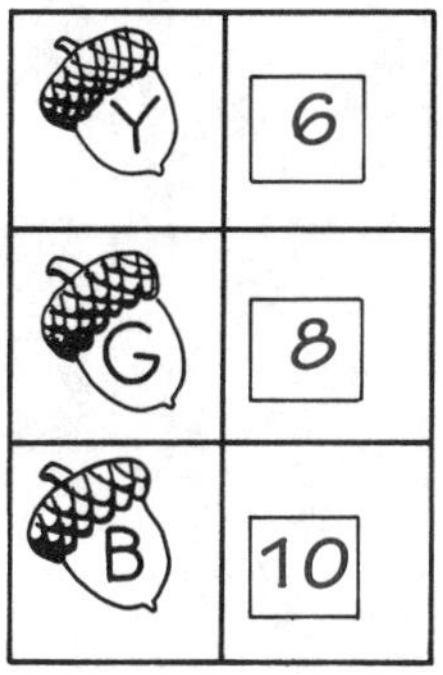

Lesson 50 Side1

50

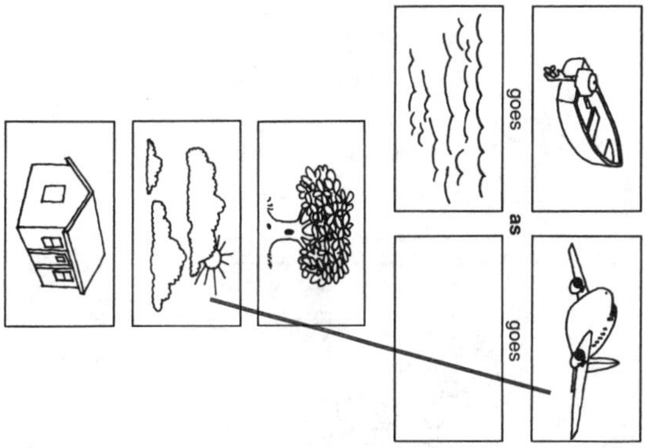

Side 2 Lesson 50

Name ______________________________

51

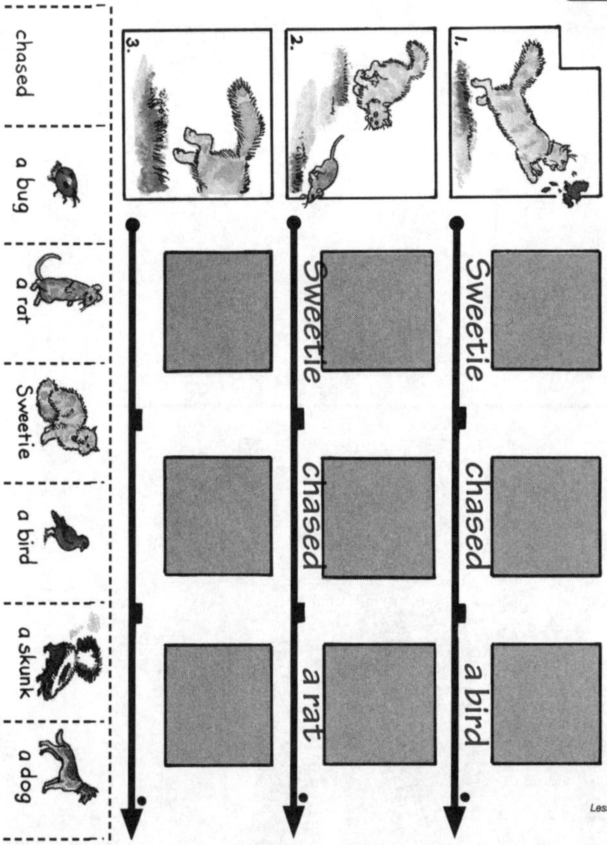

Lesson 51

Name ______________________________

52

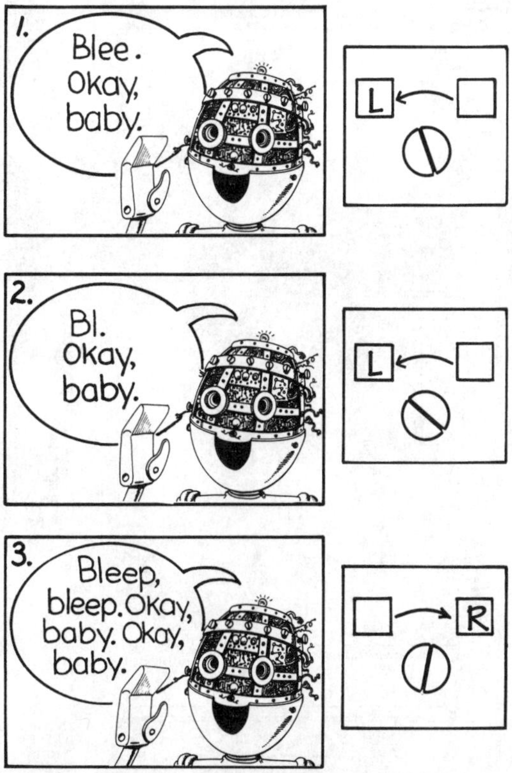

Lesson 52 Side 1

52

green or purple tables

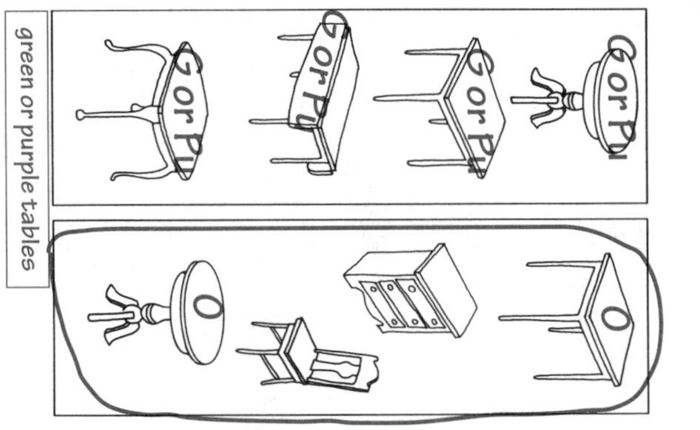

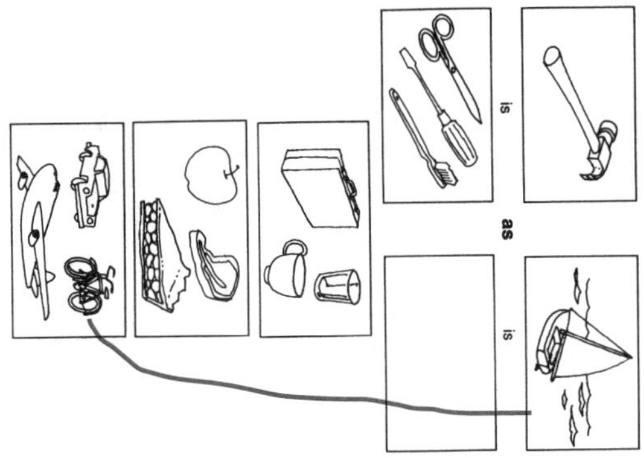

53

Name ______________________

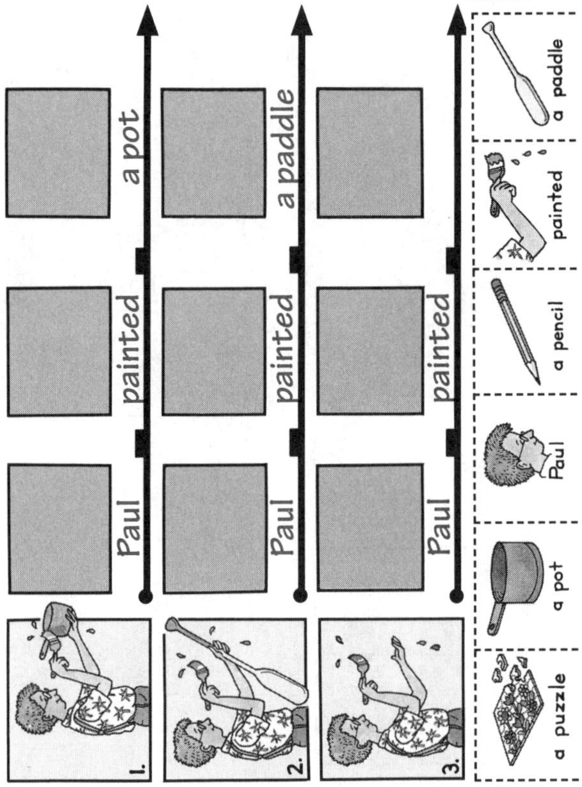

54

Name ______________________

54

blue north arrows
red east arrows

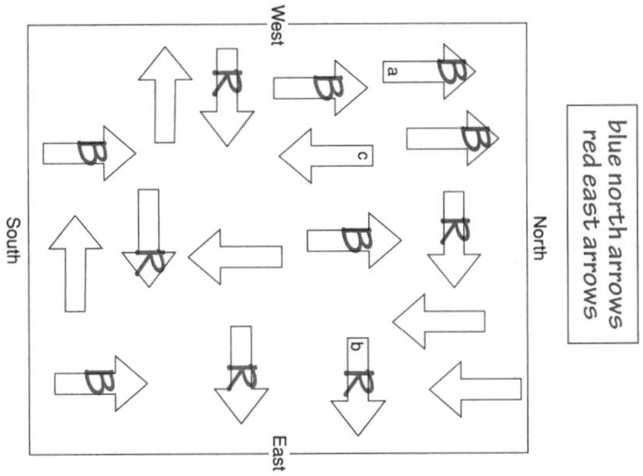

green rubber objects

Name _____

Children compose final sentence.

Clarabelle climbed a ladder

Roxie climbed a ladder

climbed a ladder

1. 2. 3.

Clarabelle — a tree — a ladder — Paul — climbed — Sweetie — Roxie

---

Name _____

Okay, baby.

25

---

black west arrows, green north arrows

North

West   East

South

Br or B

Y   Y

Br or B

brown or blue animals

Name _____

R   P   B   C   S

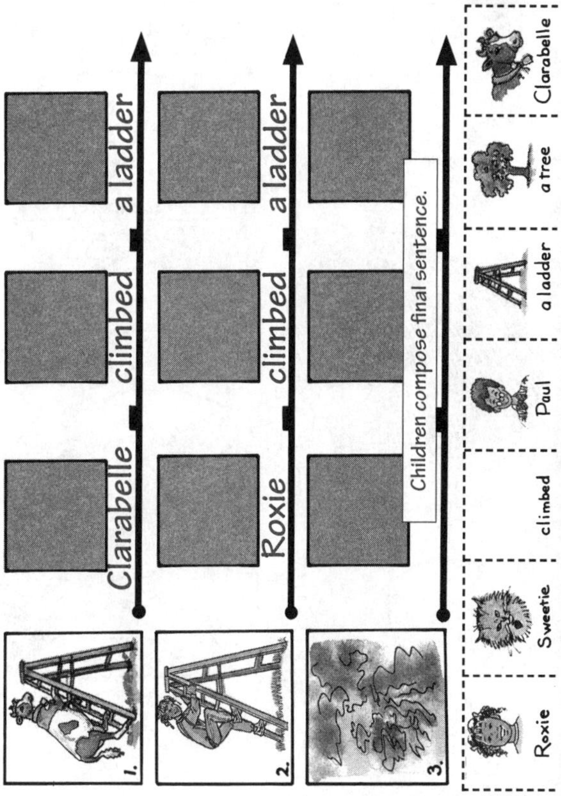

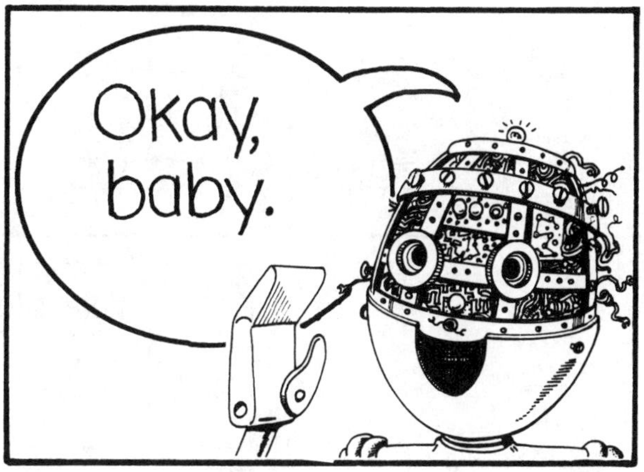

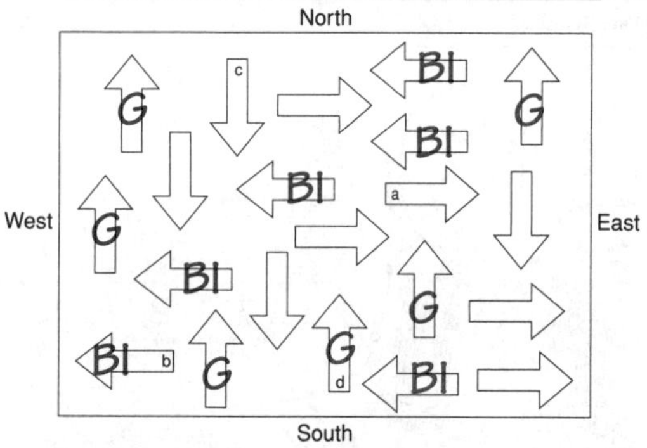

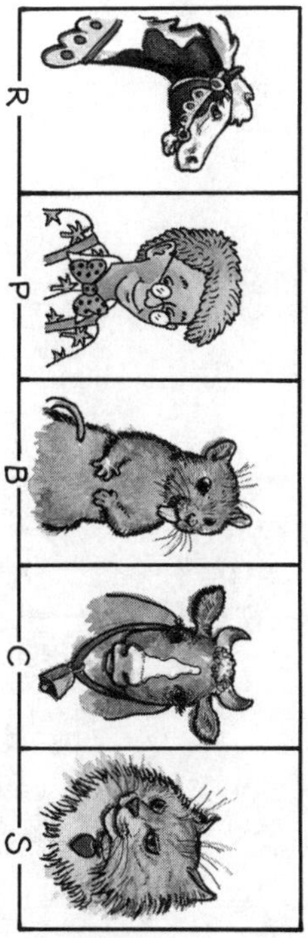

1. _____ C
2. _____ R
3. _____ P
4. _____ S
5. _____ B
6. _____ P

57

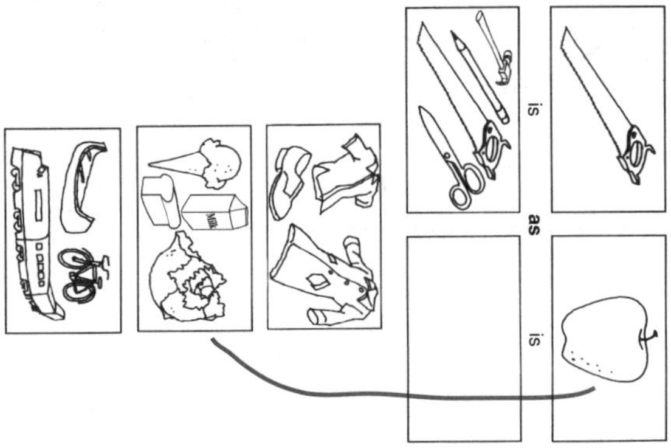

Name ______________________

58

Sunday	Monday	Tuesday	Wednesday

58

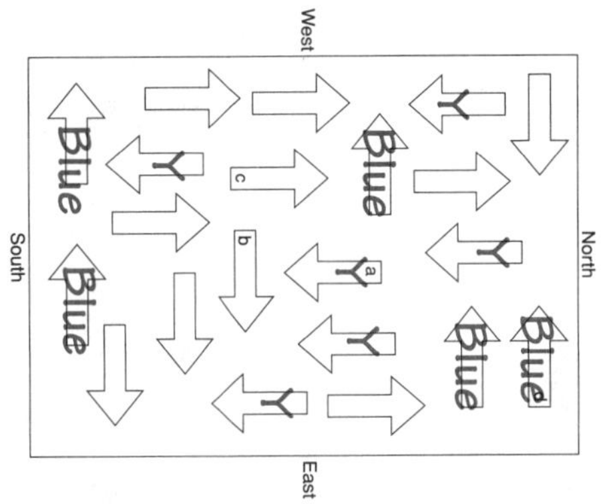

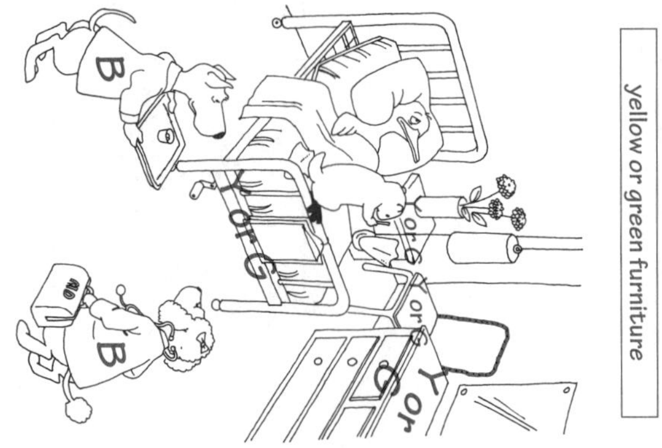

Name ______________________

59

Wednesday	Thursday	Friday	Saturday

"Why did you say __blurp__, Bleep?"

Sunday
Sunday

Monday
Monday

Tuesday
Tuesday

Wednesday
Wednesday

Thursday
Thursday

Blurpday
Friday

Saturday
Saturday

Lesson 60

Children compose final sentence and illustrate.

Paul   kissed   Clarabelle

Bleep   kissed   Molly

kissed

Clarabelle	Molly	Andrea	Bleep	Paul	Honey	kissed

Lesson 61   Side 1

27

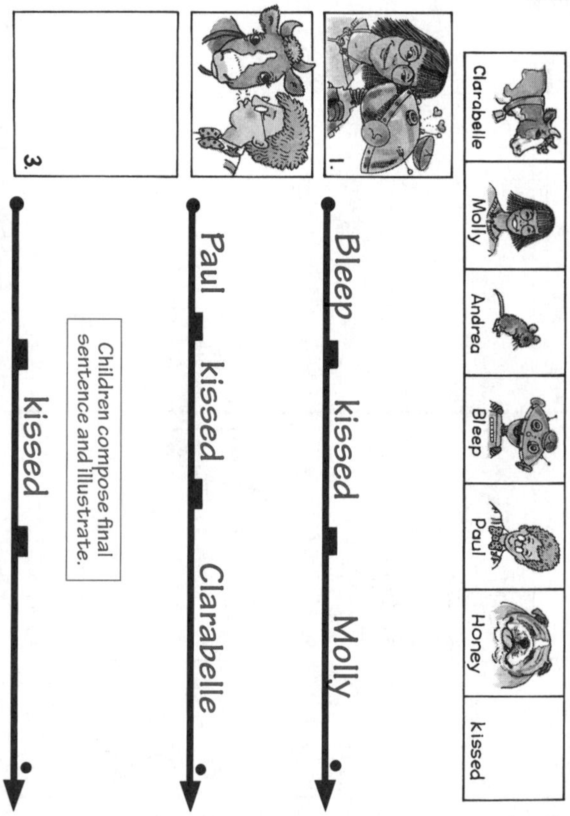

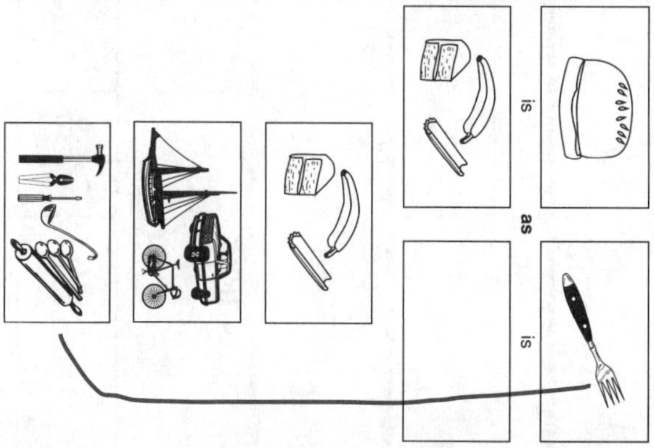

purple plums, purple and pink ladder

62

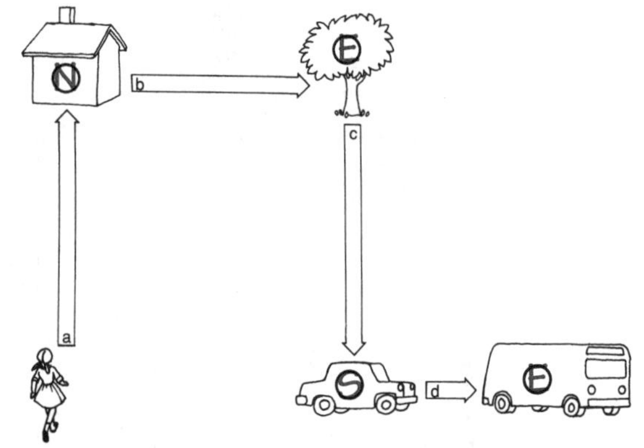

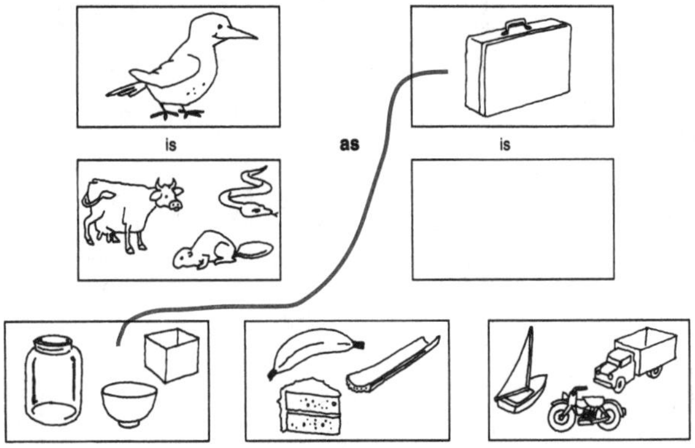

Name ____________________

63

63

black and blue motorcycles

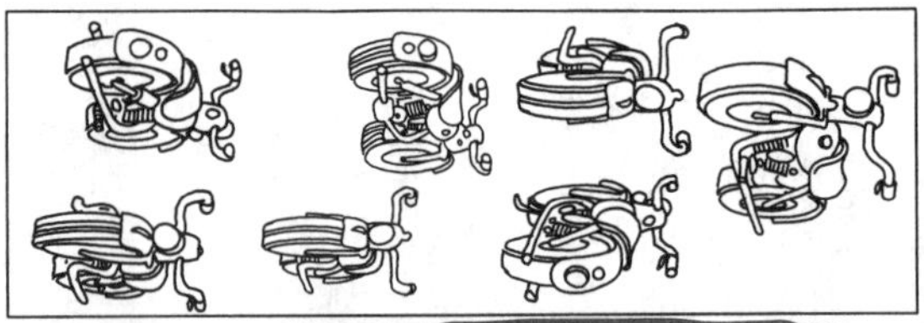

green and blue motorcycles

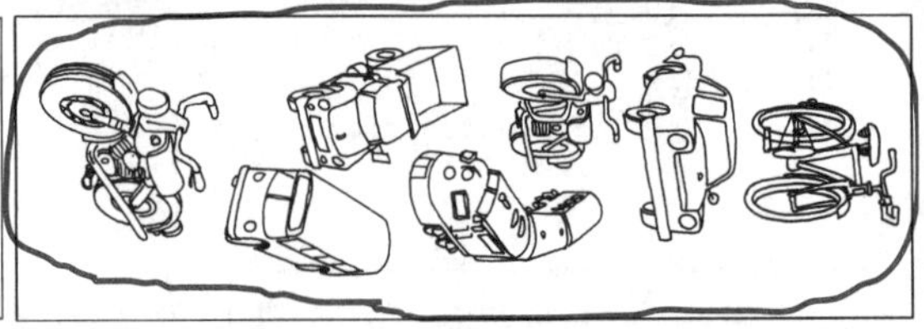

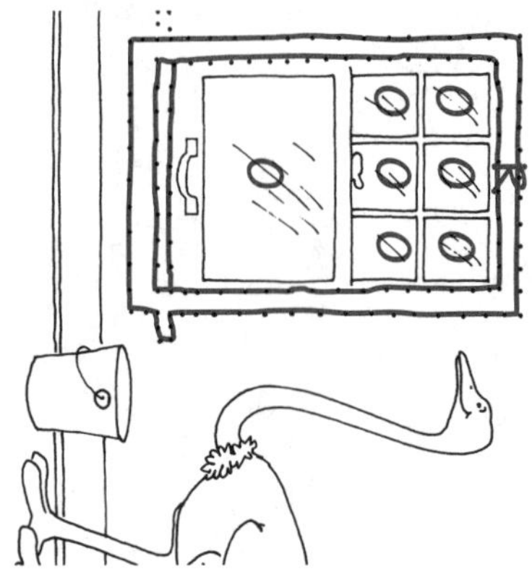

Name ____________________

64

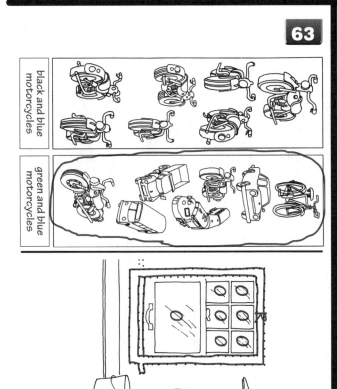

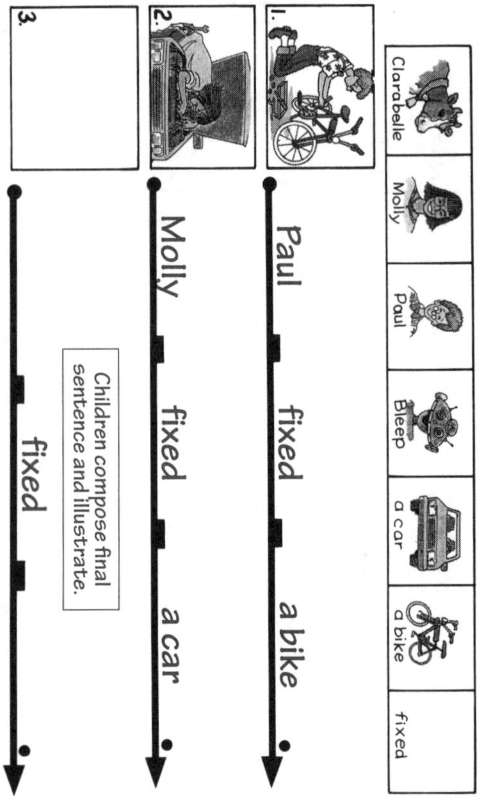

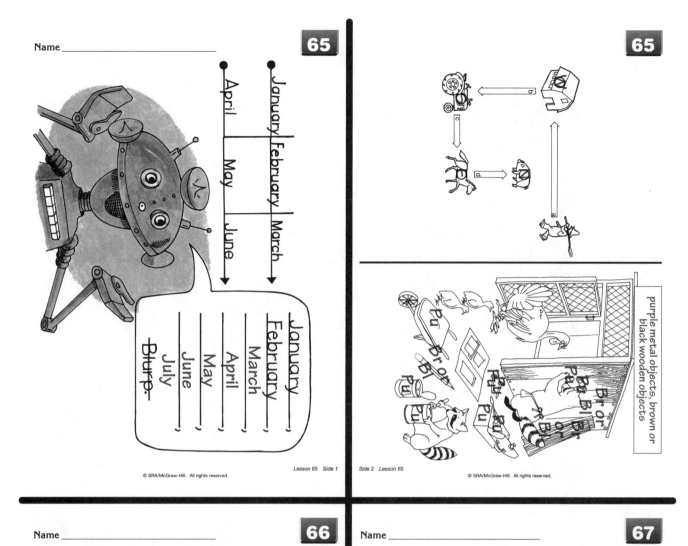

Name ________________________________

65

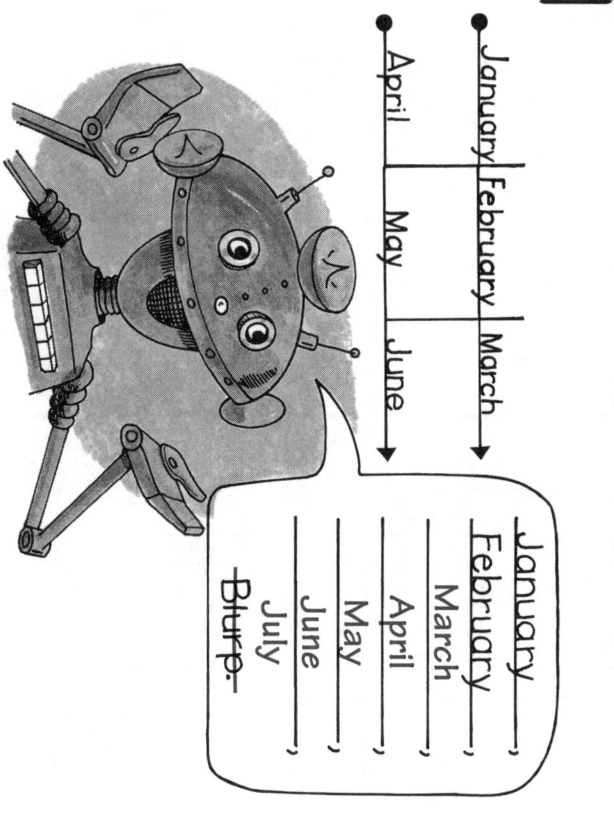

January
February
March
April
May
June
January,
February,
March,
April,
May,
June,
July,
Blurp.

65

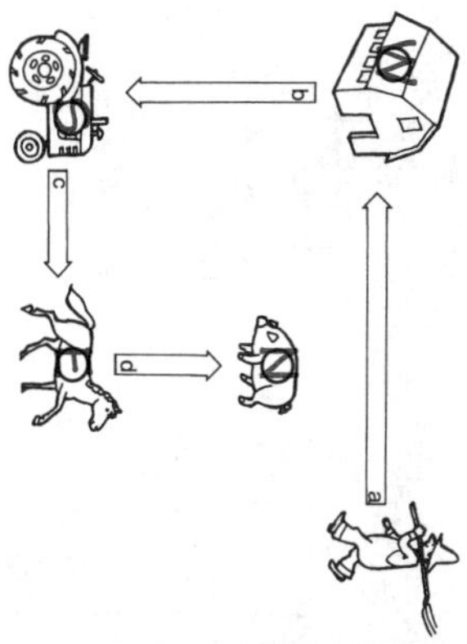

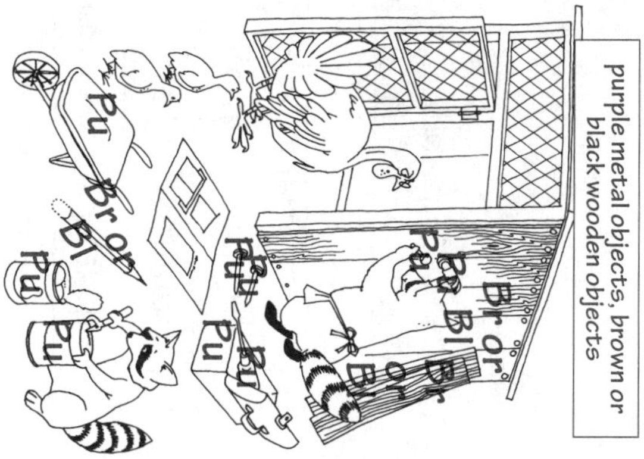

purple metal objects, brown or black wooden objects

Name ________________________________

66

January	February	March
April	May	June
July	August	September
October	November	December

September			
March	June	February	May
November	January	April	July
October	August	December	

Name ________________________________

67

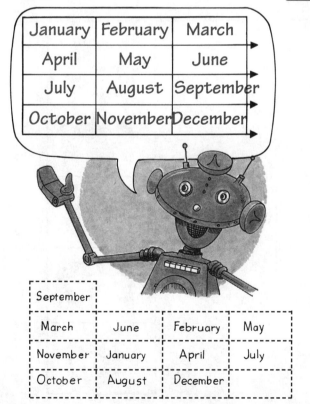

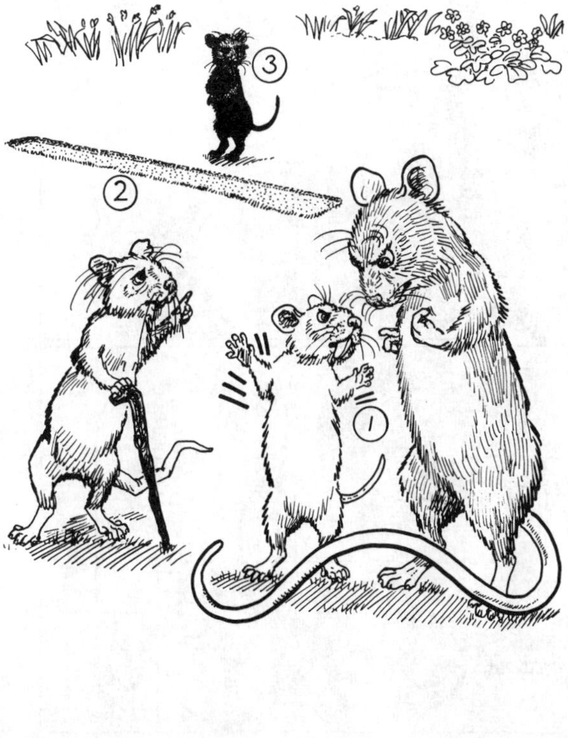

Name ______________________________

68

January
February
March
April
May
June
July
August
September
October
November
December

68

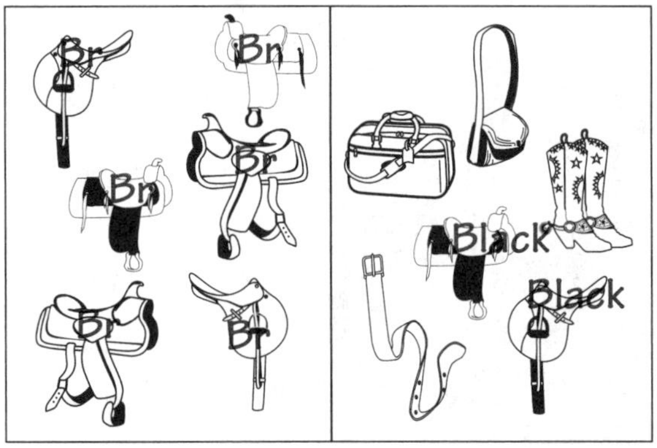

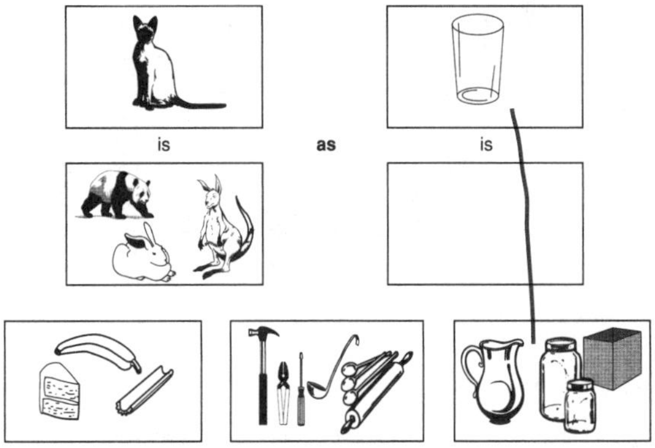

is
as
is

Name ______________________________

69

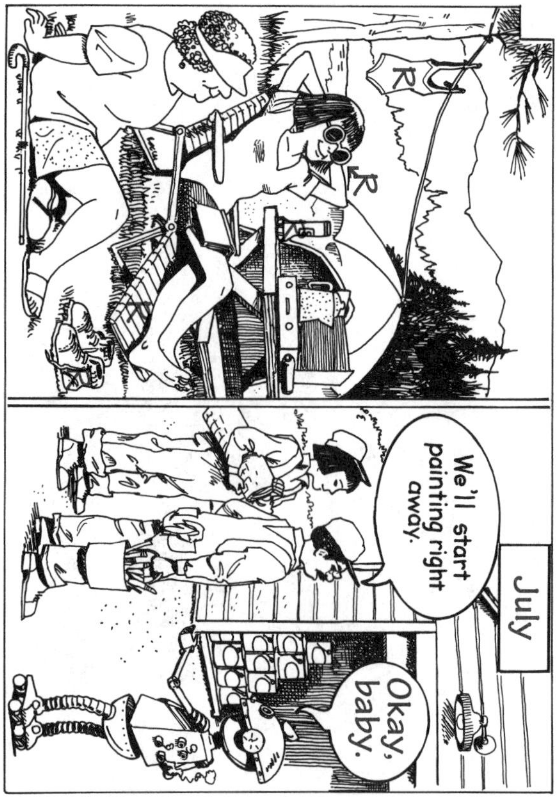

R
R
July
We'll start painting right away.
Okay, baby.

Name ______________________________

70

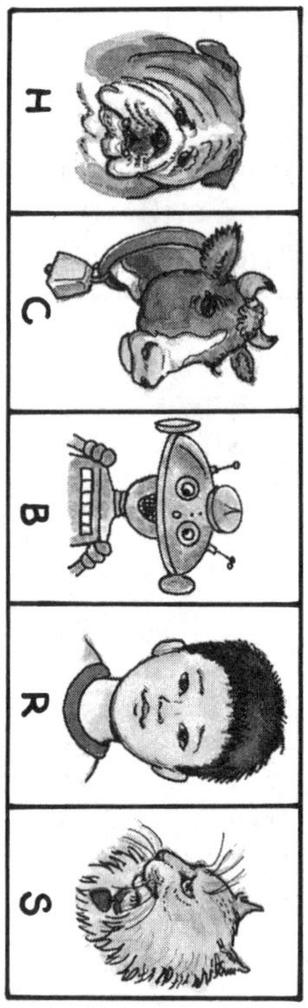

1. C
2. S
3. R
4. H
5. B

red and purple clothing

holds

as

holds

Name _____

1.

2.

3.

4.

Name _____

B   S   R   M

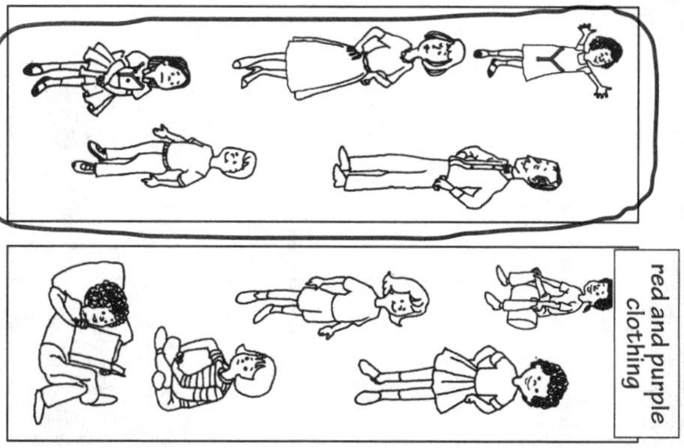

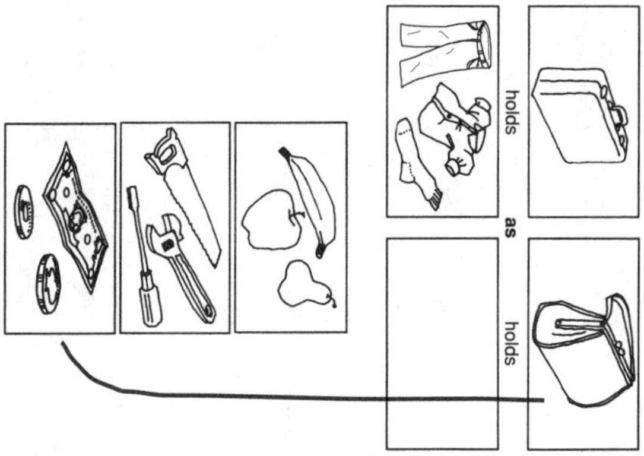

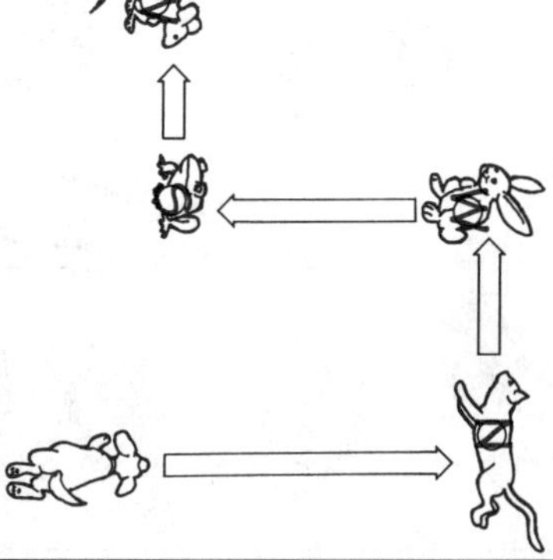

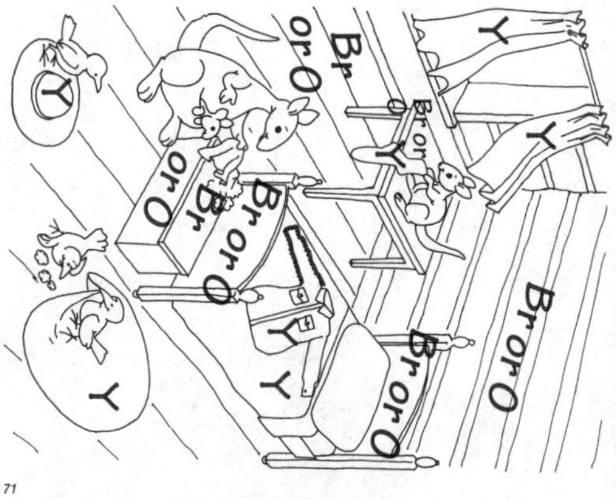

1. _____ R _____
2. _____ S _____
3. _____ M _____
4. _____ B _____
5. _____ R _____

72

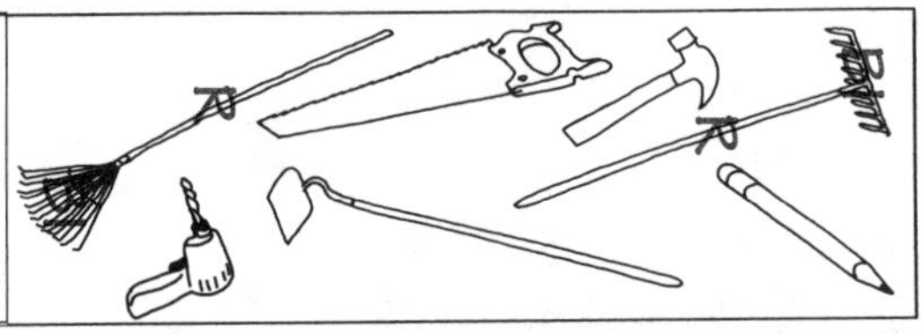

rakes black with red handles

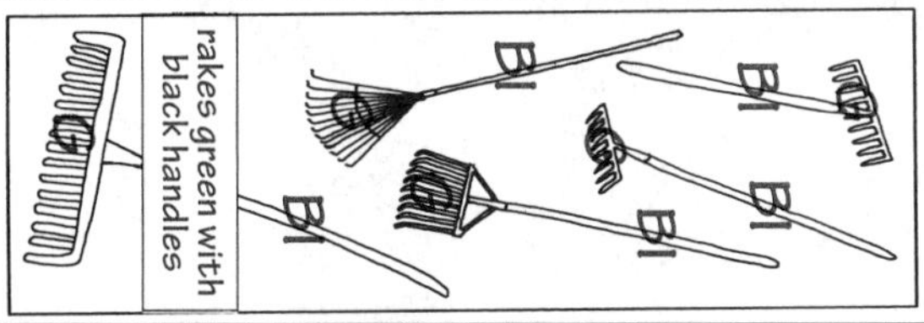

rakes green with black handles

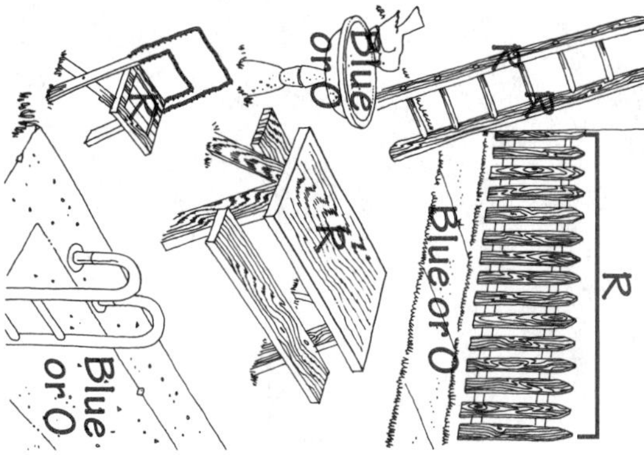

Side 2 Lesson 72

73

Name ______________________

1. Paul fell off a bike.
2. Bleep fell off a ladder.
3. Children compose final sentence and illustrate.

Lesson 73

74

Name ______________________

1. Roger sat on a chair.
2. Clarabelle sat on a bed.
3. Children compose final sentence and illustrate.

Lesson 74 Side 1

74

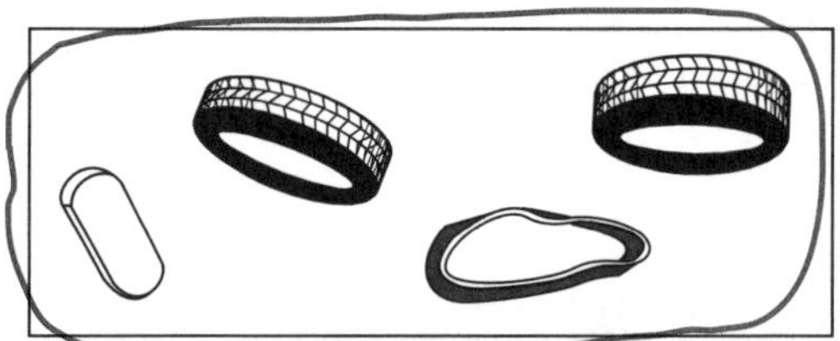

black and blue tires

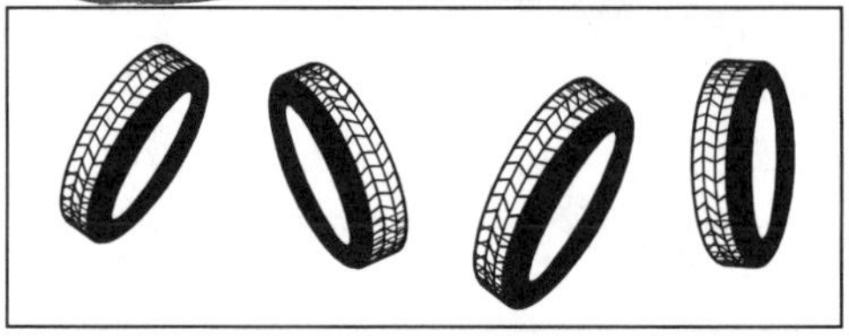

black tires

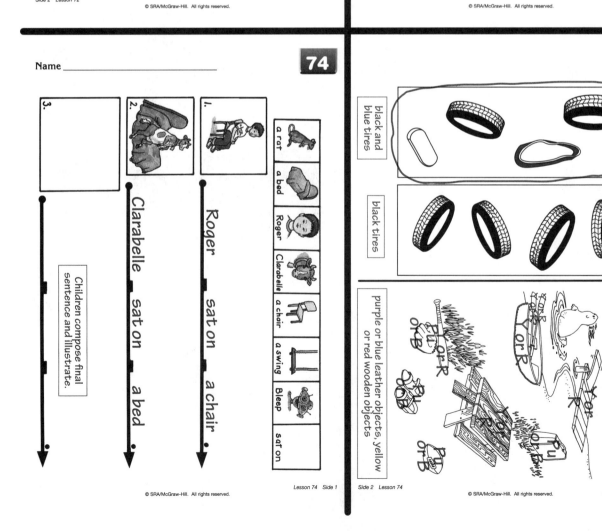

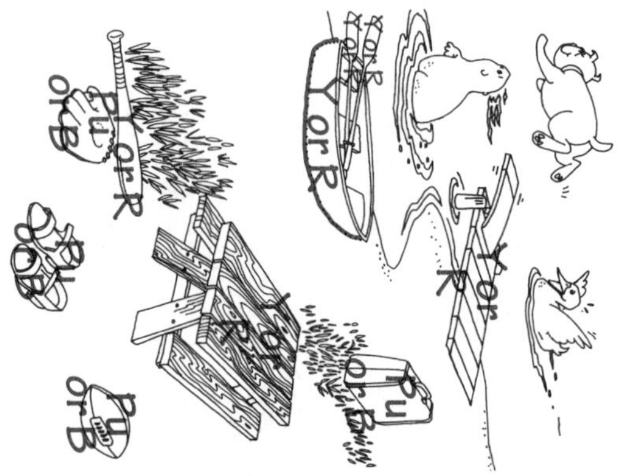

purple or blue leather objects, yellow or red wooden objects

Side 2 Lesson 74

Name ______________________________

75

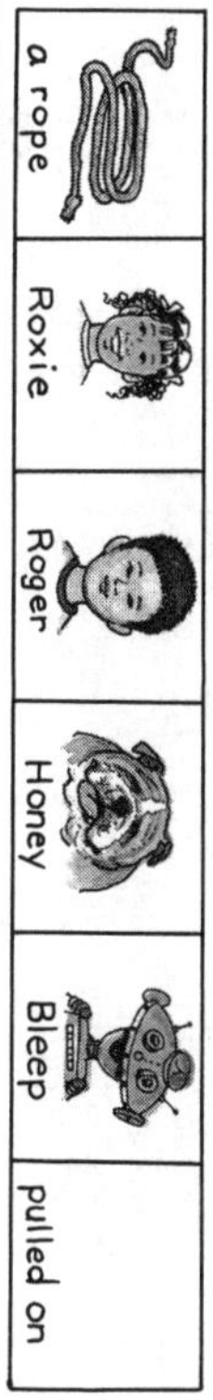

1. Honey pulled on a rope.
2. Roxie pulled on Honey.
3. Children choose own subject here. pulled on Roxie.

Lesson 75 Side 1

75

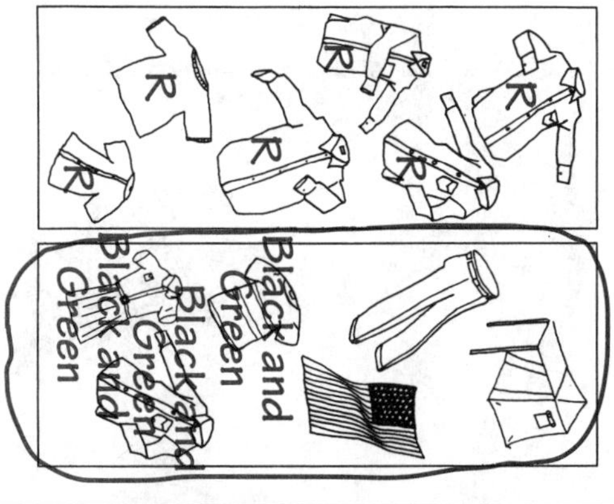

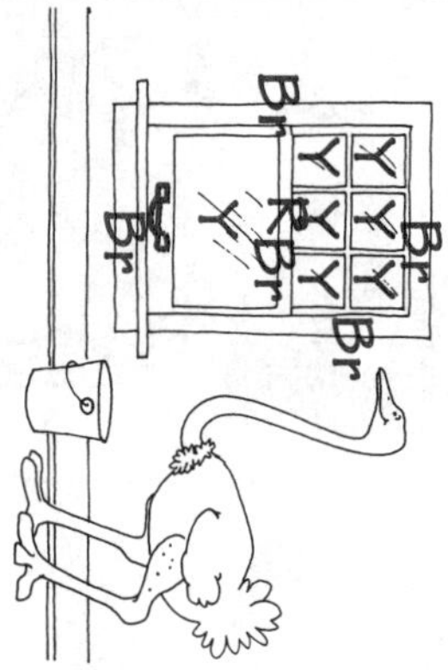

brown window frame, yellow pane, red lock

Side 2 Lesson 75

Name ______________________________

76

1. Sweetie jumped over a mouse.
2. Honey jumped over Sweetie.
3. Children choose own subject here. jumped over Honey.

Lesson 76 Side 1

76

saws yellow with brown handles

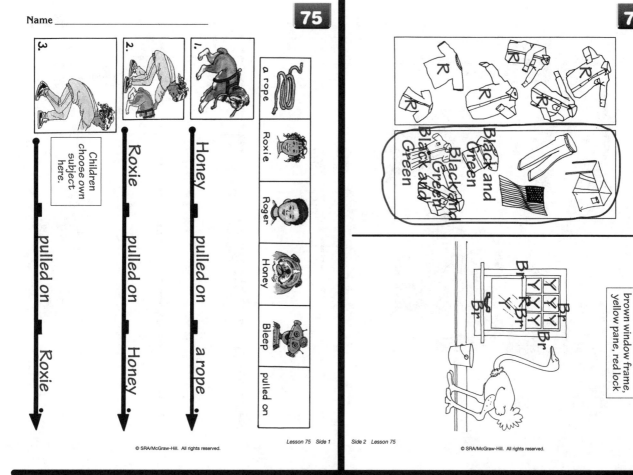

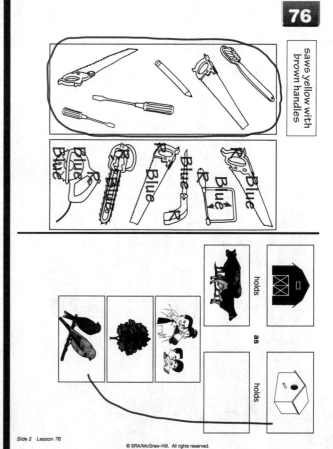

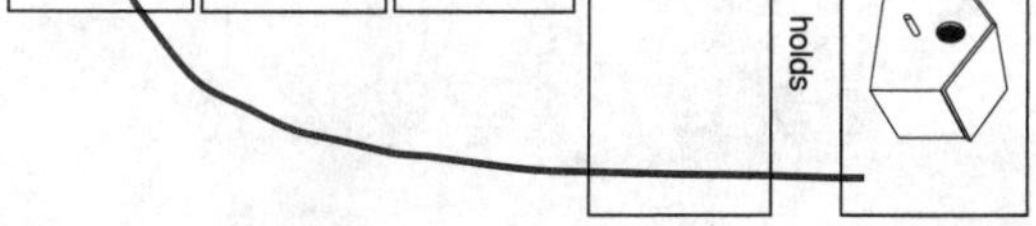

Side 2 Lesson 76

yellow cat and
reflection

Lesson 77

| rocks | Sweetie | Honey | skunks | hats | carried | paint |

1. Roxie

2. Paul

3. Clarabelle

Roxie ———————— carried ———————— rocks

Paul ———————— carried ———————— paint

Clarabelle ———————— carried

Children
choose own
subject
here.

Lesson 78

34

yellow cat and
reflection

Lesson 79

| cone | the | fox |

The fox had a bone.

The ram had a cone.

_____

_____

Lesson 80 Side 1

80

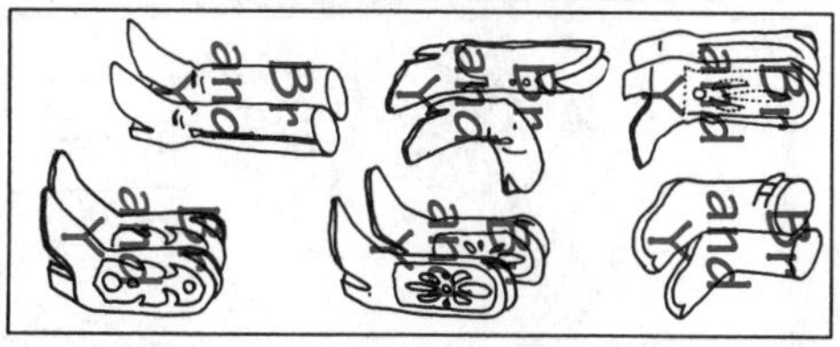

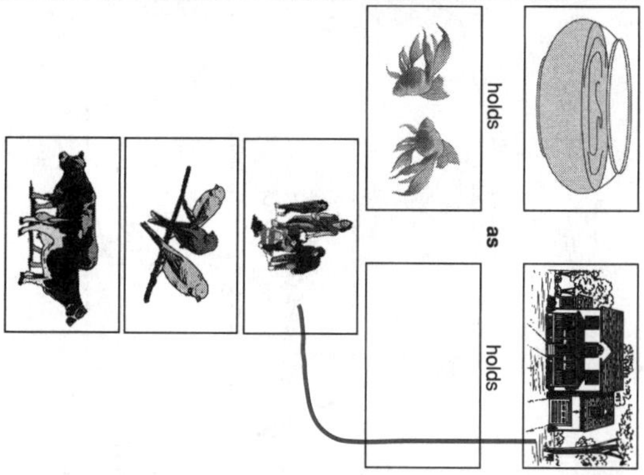

Name ______________________

81

cake fox

The fox had a cake.

The ram had a rake.

81

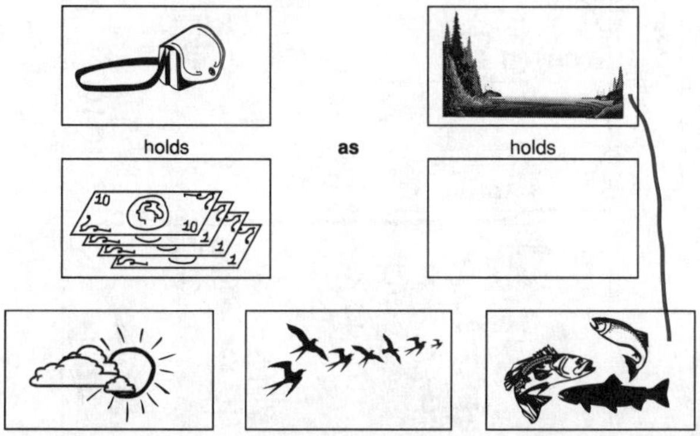

Name ______________________

82

A.

Name ____________________

83

fish bird under coat

The fish is under a boat.

The bird is under a coat.

83

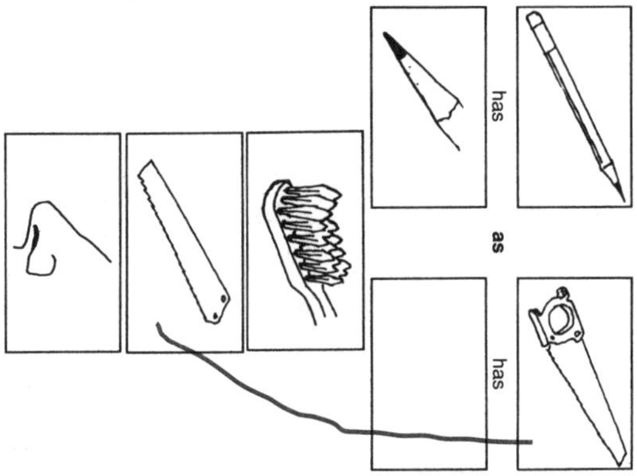

Name ____________________

84

hat

The man had a bat.

The ram had a hat.

84

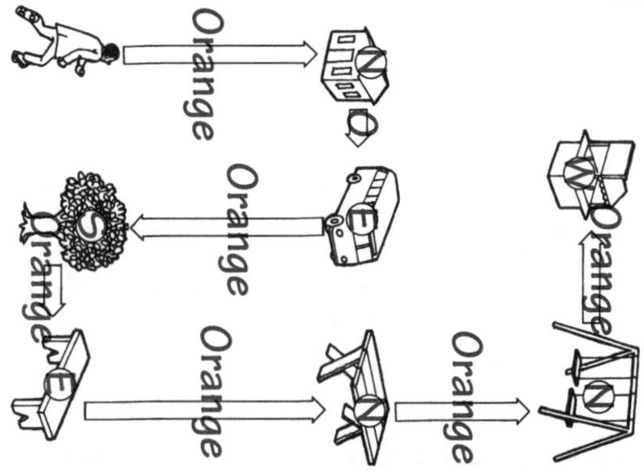

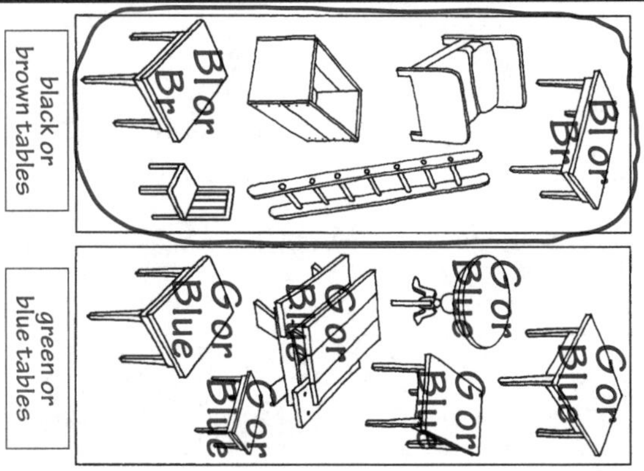

Name _____

Lesson 85   Side 1

Lesson 85   Side 2

37

Name _____

car   toad   bug

The car is on a road.
The bug is on a toad.

Lesson 86   Side 1

Side 2   Lesson 86

blue or red metal objects,
orange plastic objects

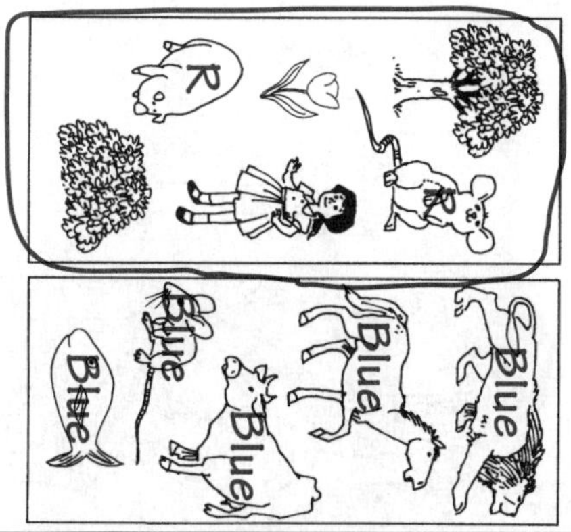

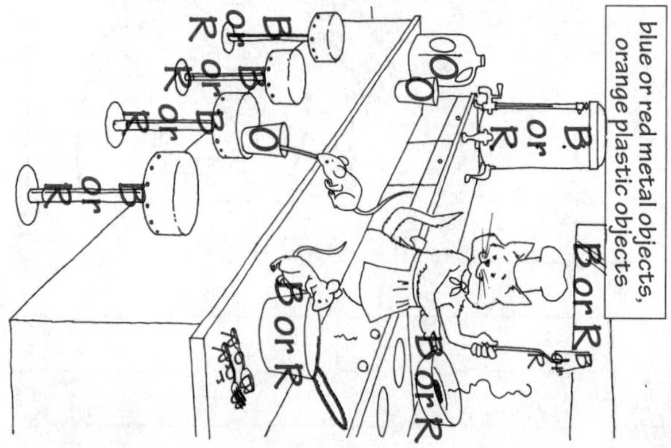

Name ______________________

87

his	her	socks	shoes	feet

His feet had socks.

Her feet had shoes.

87

P	Pink rocks	9
B	Brown rocks	6
G	Gray rocks	10
	Other rocks	9

Name ______________________

88

bird	man

The bird is on a van.

The bug is on a man.

88

Name ______________________

89

mole under coat

The mole is under a goat.

The rat is under a coat.

89

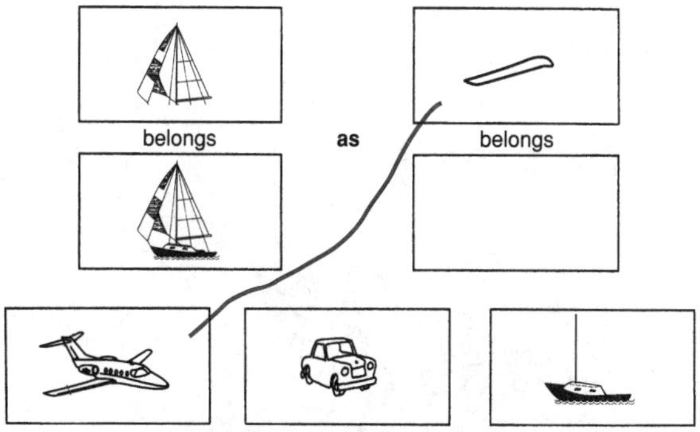

food vehicles

 vehicles

 food

 food

 vehicles

Name ______________________

90

ant cake

The ant is in a cake.

The goat is in a lake.

90

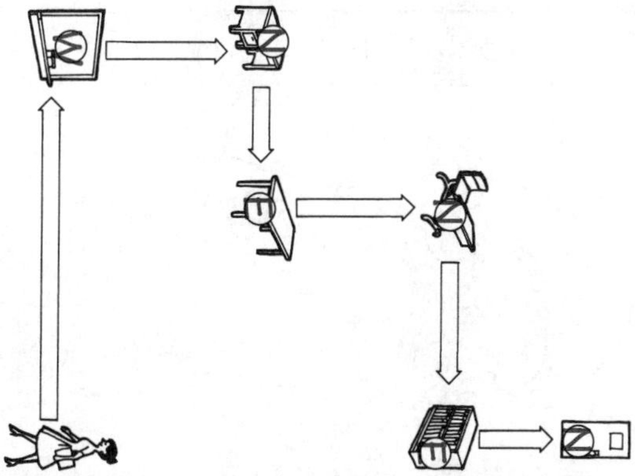

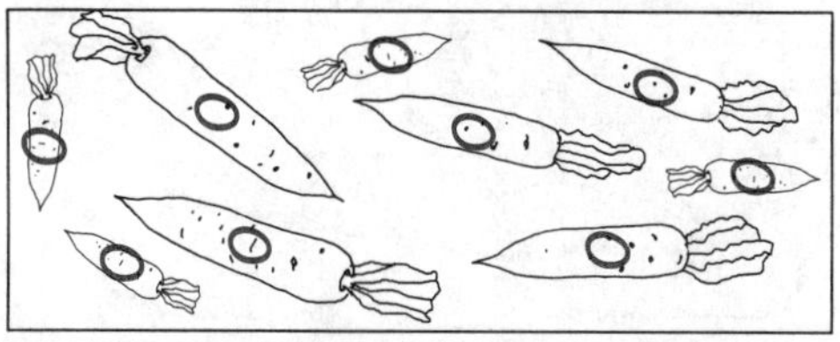

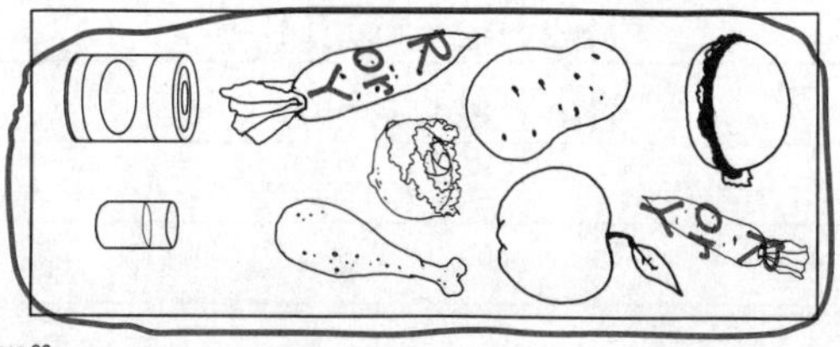

Name ____________________

91

clock will sing

The man will sing.

The clock will ring.

91

Name ____________________

92

baby plane cry

The plane will fly.

The baby will cry.

92

Name ____________________

93

mail

The man had mail.

The cat had a pail.

93

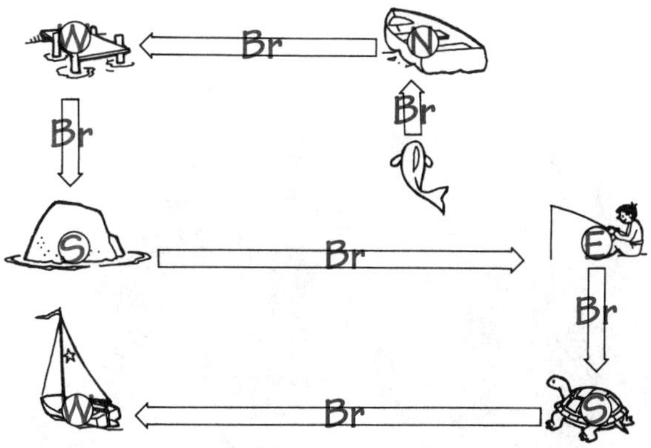

containers furniture

 containers

 containers

 furniture

 containers

 furniture

Name ____________________

94

94

woman rock

The woman had a ring.

The man had a rock.

Name ______________________________

95

Lesson 95 Side 1

95

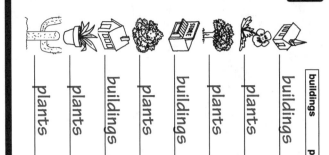

buildings	plants

buildings
plants
plants
buildings
plants
buildings
plants
plants

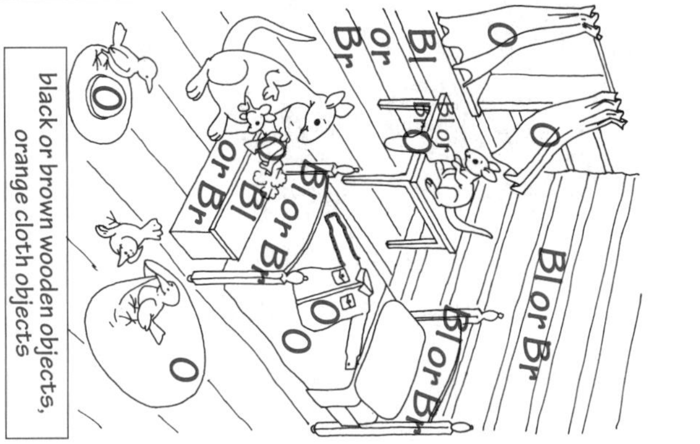

Side 2 Lesson 95

Name ______________________________

96

short	boat	sail

The cat had a short tail.

The boat had a big sail.

____

____

Lesson 96 Side 1

96

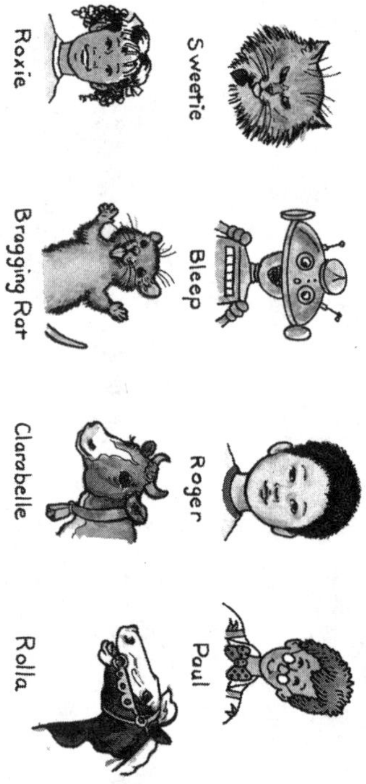

Side 2 Lesson 96

Name ______________________________

97

1.
2.
3.
4.
5.
6.
7.
8.

97

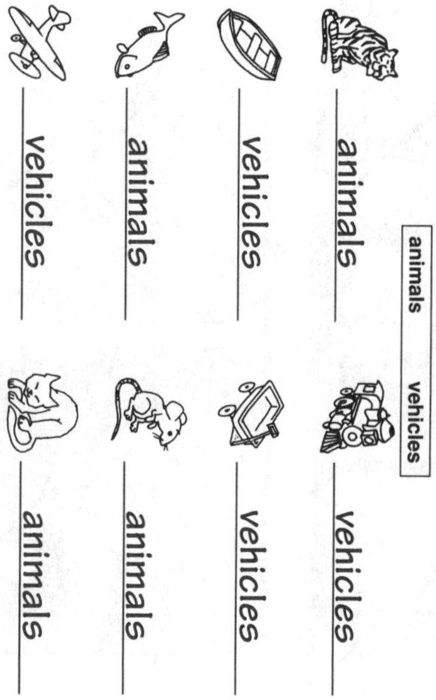

vehicles
animals
vehicles
animals
animals
vehicles
animals
animals
vehicles
vehicles

Name ______________________________

98

girl	boy	sock

The boy had a sock.

The girl had a hat.

98

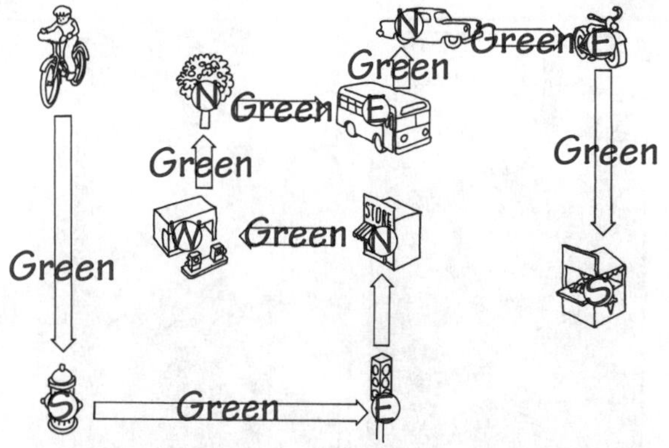

Green
Green
Green
Green
Green
Green
Green
Green

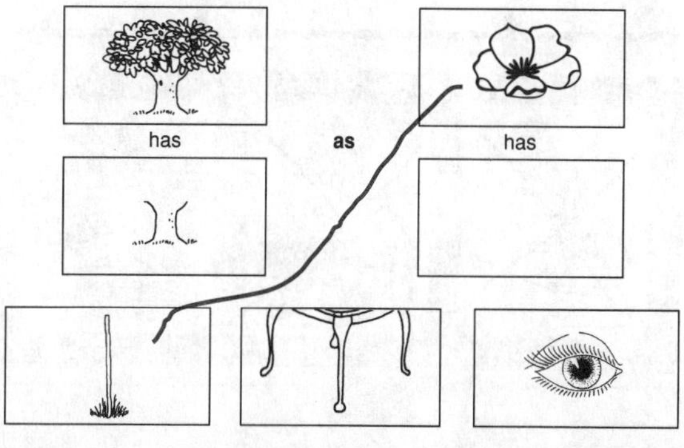

has
as
has

Name ______________________

99

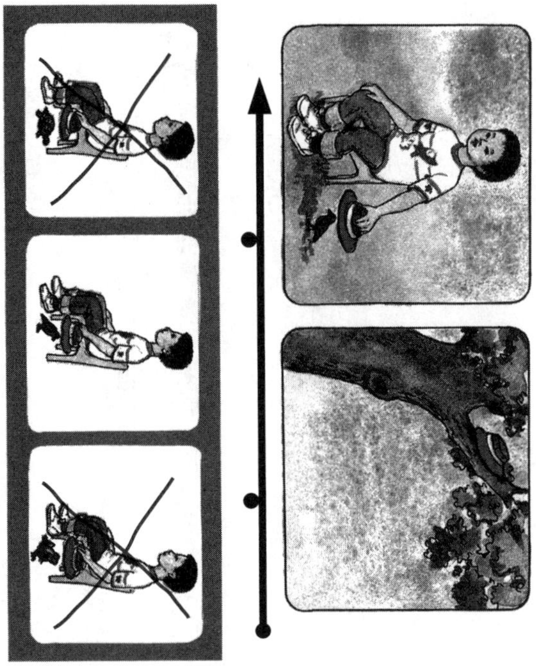

99

swim

The girl will run.

The boy will swim.

Name ______________________

100

100

girl drink eat boy

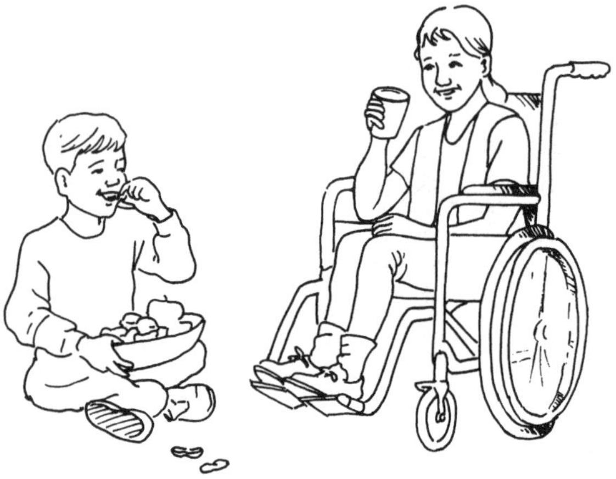

The boy will eat.

The girl will drink.

Name ______________________________

101

stick

The pig had a stick.

The cat had a cup.

Lesson 101 Side 1

101

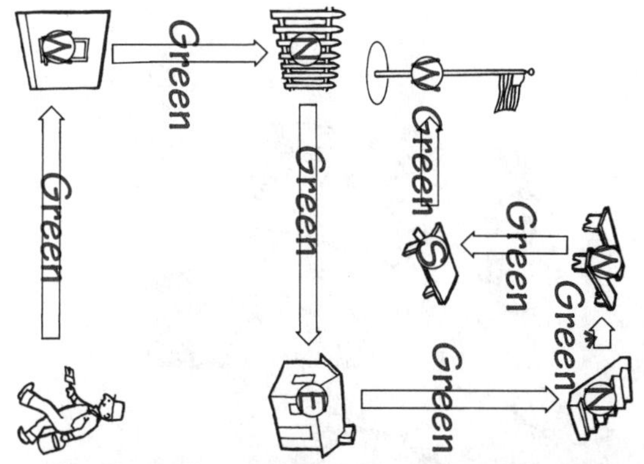

green or blue clothes

purple or yellow clothes

Side 2 Lesson 101

Name ______________________________

102

fish cow car

The cow had a car.

The fish had a hat.

Lesson 102 Side 1

102

furniture plants

furniture

plants

plants

furniture

furniture

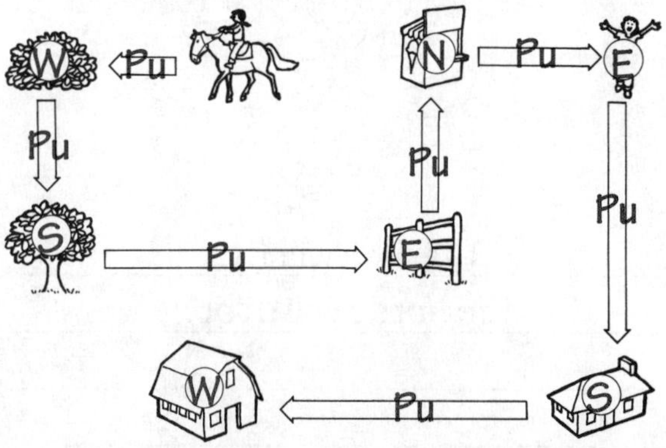

Side 2 Lesson 102

Name ______________________________

103

bird	fly	girl

The girl will sing.

The bird will fly.

103

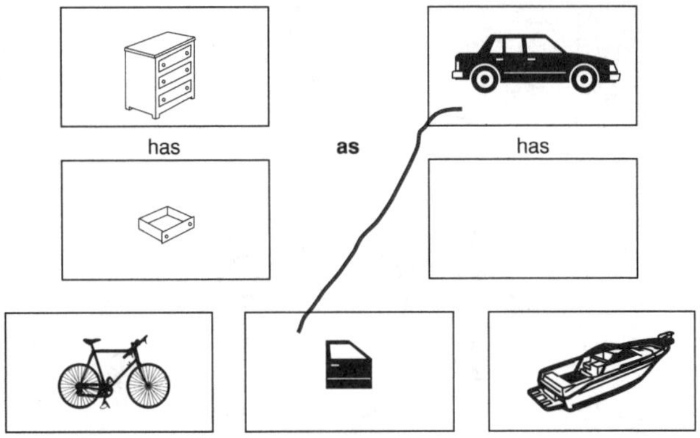

clothing	buildings

 clothing

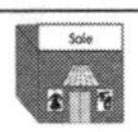 buildings

 buildings

 clothing

 clothing

 clothing

 buildings

 buildings

Name ______________________________

104

stop	horse	fly

The man will fly.

The horse will stop.

104

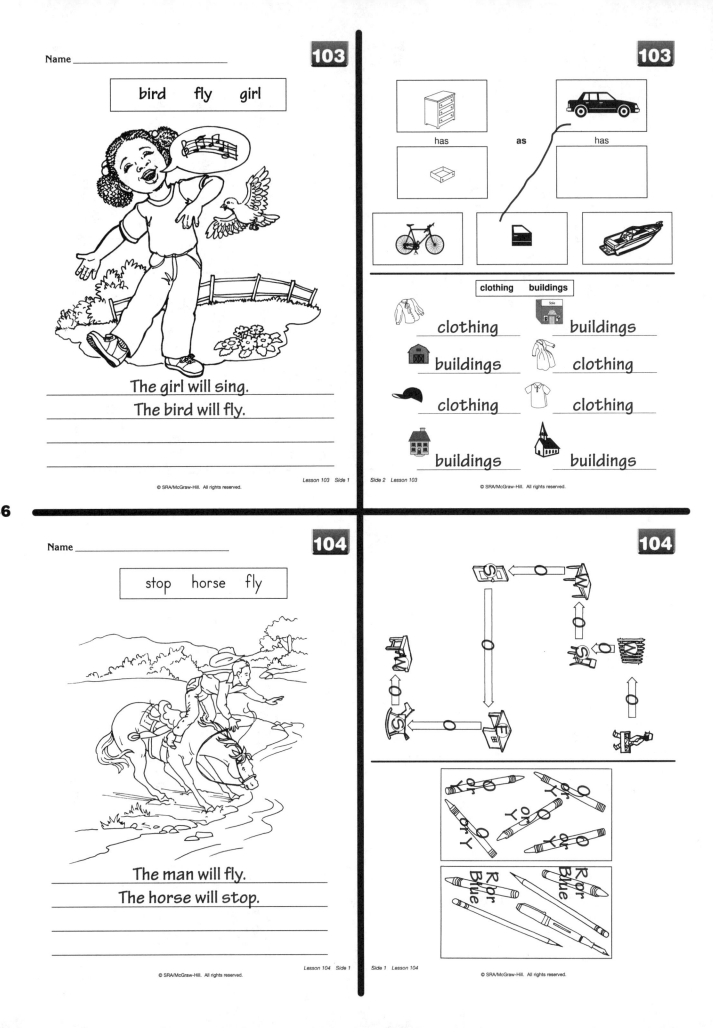

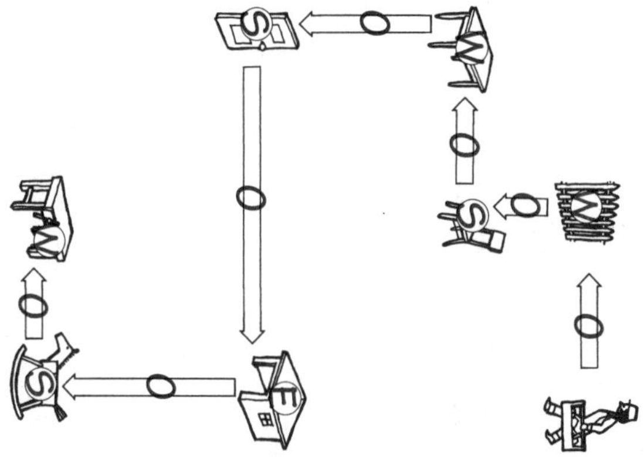

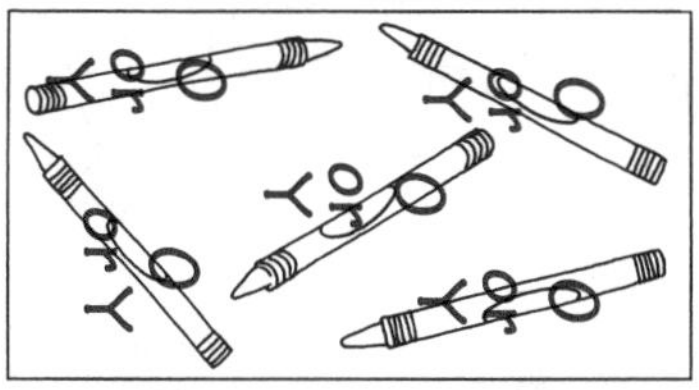

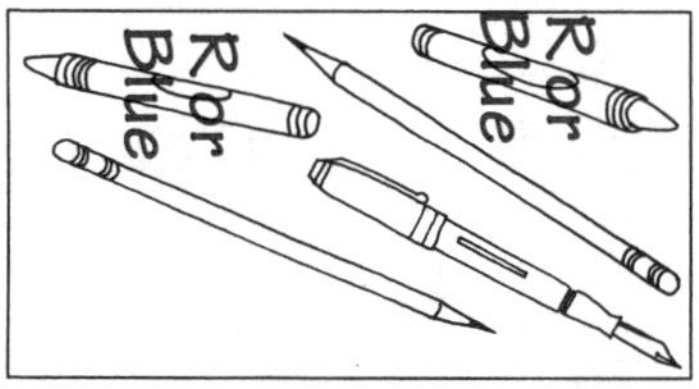

Name ______________________

105

mole dig

The mole will dig.

The fox will sit.

Side 1 Lesson 105

105

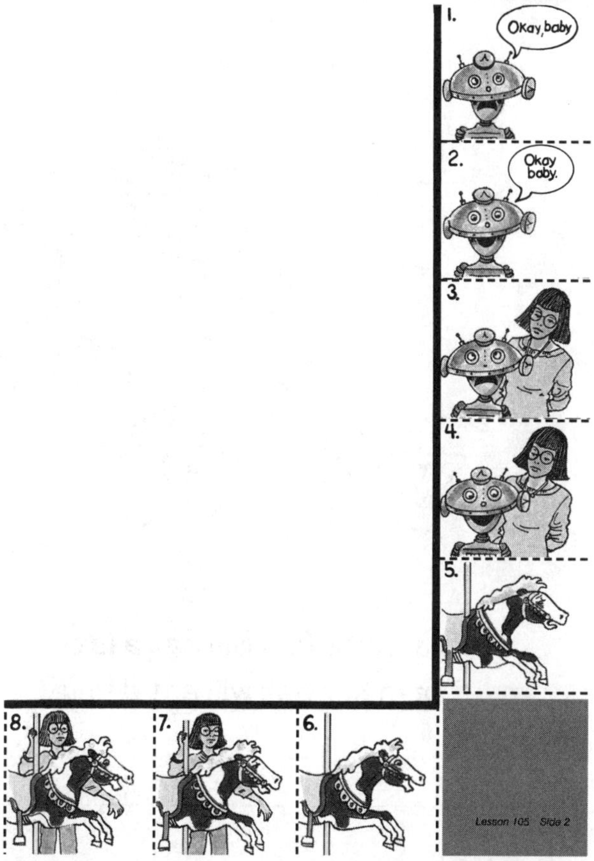

Lesson 105 Side 2

Name ______________________

106

cow walk

The cow will walk.

The cat will sit.

Lesson 106 Side 1

106

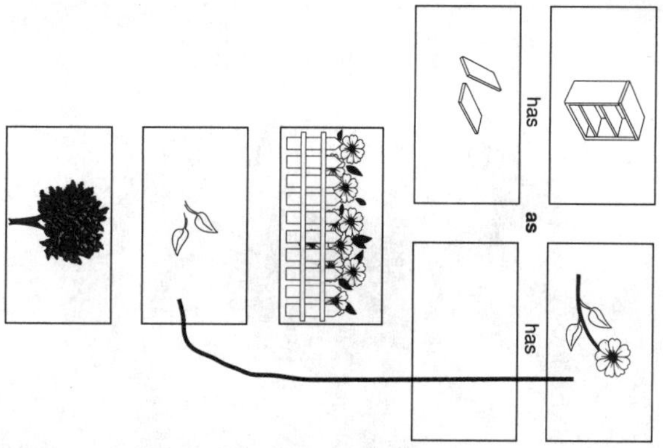

purple or black leather items,
yellow metal items

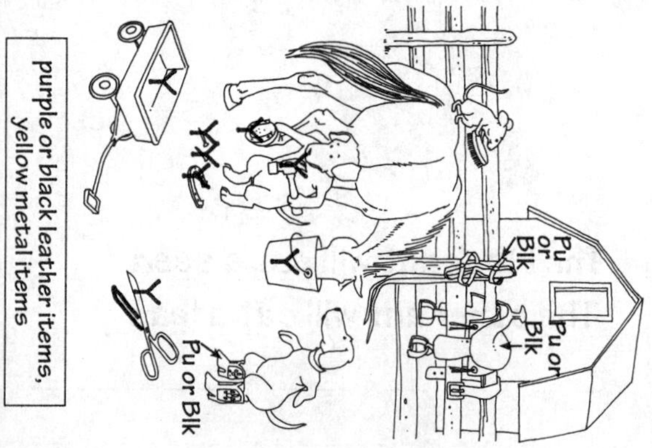

Side 2 Lesson 106

Name ______________________________

107

eat white leaf other

The white fish will eat a leaf.

The other fish will eat a bug.

107

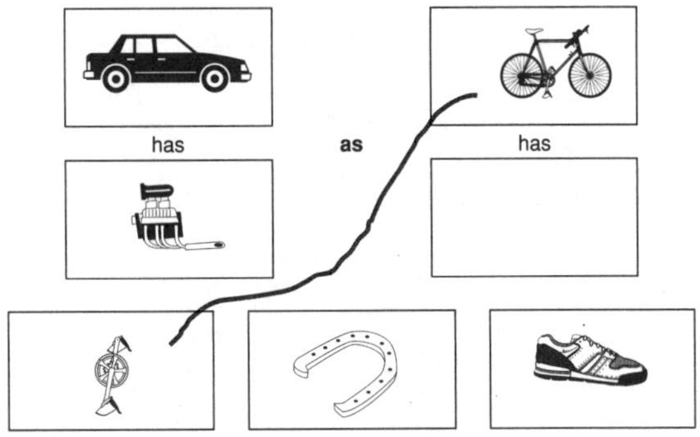

vehicles containers

 vehicles

 vehicles

 containers

 containers

 containers

 vehicles

 vehicles

 containers

Name ______________________________

108

leaf other black

The black ant will eat a seed.

The other ant will eat a leaf.

108

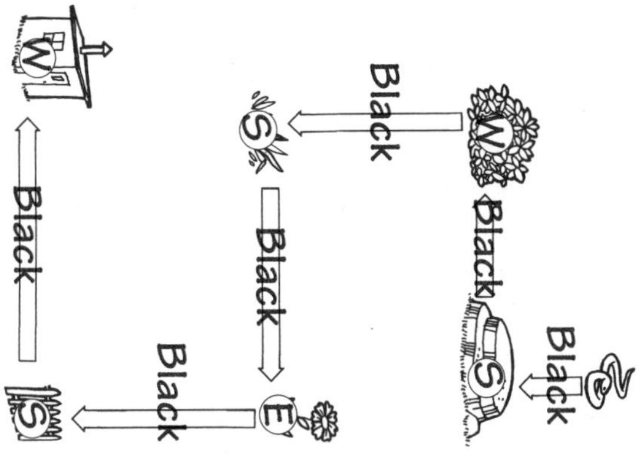

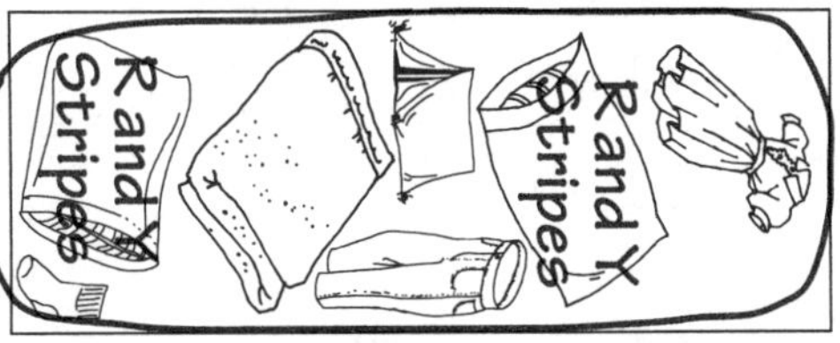

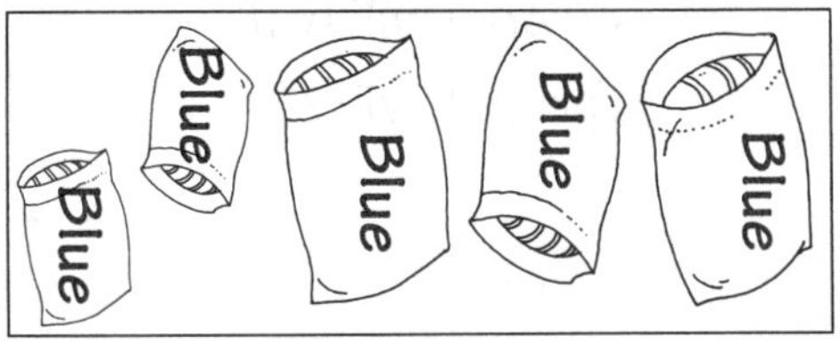

Name _____

| was | rope | rug |

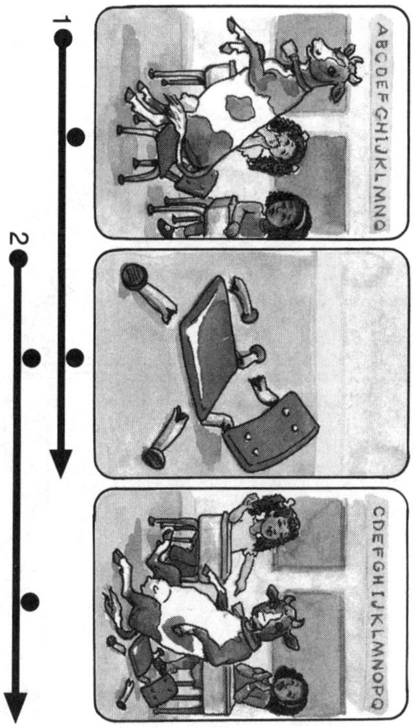

The bird was on a rope.

The bug was on a rug.

_____

_____

Lesson 109 Side 1

Side 2 Lesson 109

49

Name _____

Clarabelle	sat on	a hat	Sweetie
Paul	kissed	Molly	a rock
Bleep	painted	a pie	a rat

1. _____

2. _____

3. _____

Children compose other sentences
and illustrate one.

| vehicles | food |

vehicles   vehicles

food   vehicles

vehicles   food

food   vehicles

Blue

Blue

Blue   Blue

Blue

Blue

Blue

Blue   Blue

Lesson 110 Side 1

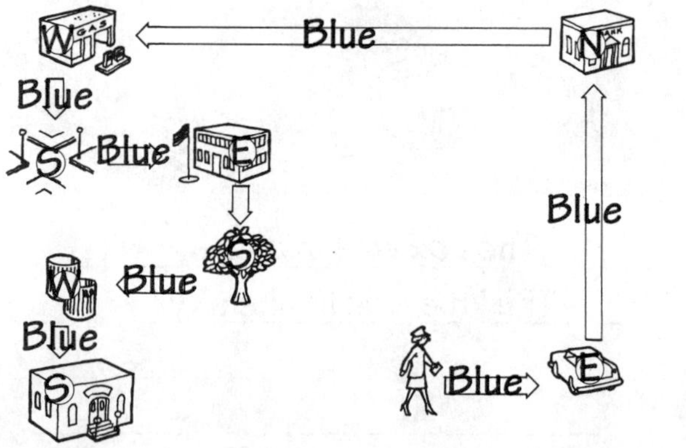

Name ______________________

111

was cow hill

The man was on a cow.

The cat was on a hill.

111

orange pencils

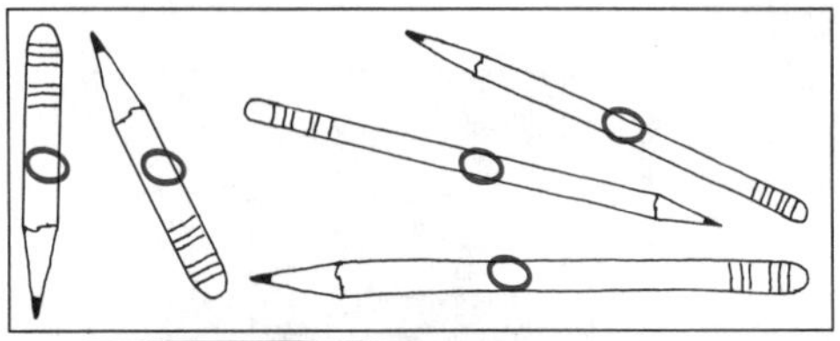

blue and green dots on pencils

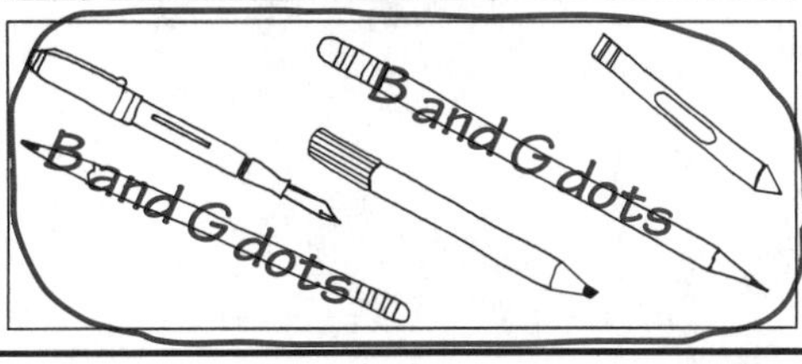

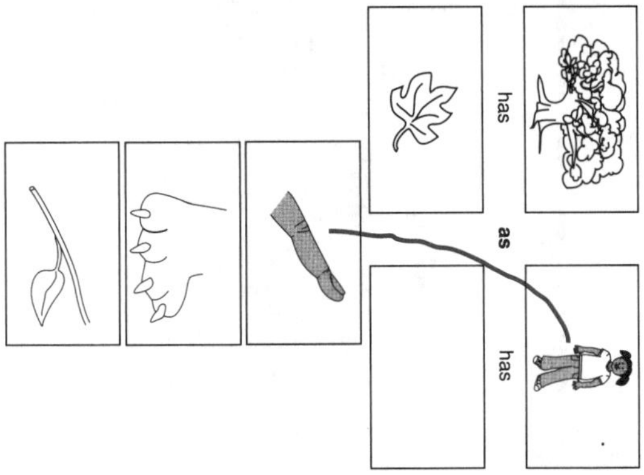

Name ______________________

112

lake sky kite

The box was in a lake.

The kite was in the sky.

112

rough tall old pull

1. push pull
2. young old
3. smooth rough
4. short tall

tools furniture plants

 tools  plants

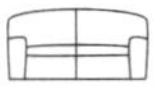 furniture  furniture

 plants  tools

 tools  plants

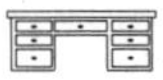 furniture  tools

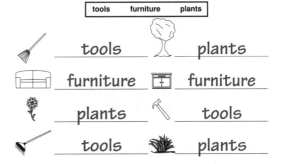

Name ______________________

113

was goat dog

The dog was on a log.

The goat was in a log.

Lesson 113 Side 1

113

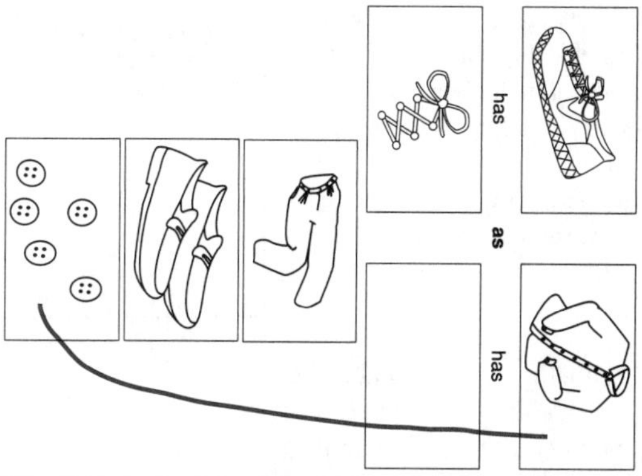

win dry short fast

1. slow fast
2. lose win
3. wet dry
4. tall short

Side 2 Lesson 112

Name ______________________

114

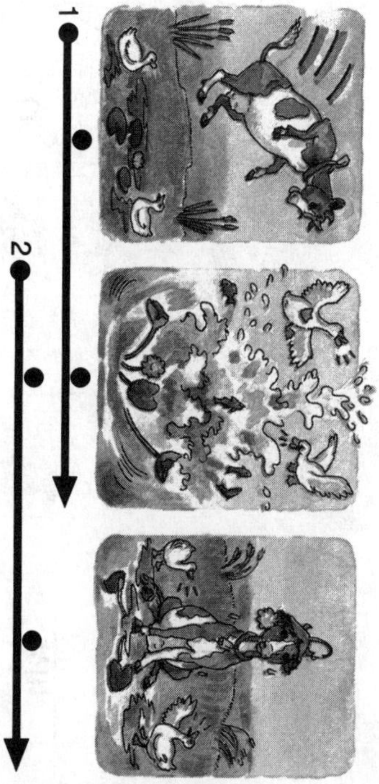

Lesson 114 Side 1

114

snake

The fish was in a lake.

The bug was on a snake.

Lesson 114 Side 2

Name ____________________ **115**

1. One day, 16 green frogs were sitting on a log that was floating in a lake. The log was near the shore of the lake, and the frogs were having a very peaceful time, just sitting and sunning and making frog sounds – "Croak, croak."

2. Clarabelle was in a field right next to the lake. She saw those happy green frogs all lined up on that floating log and she said to herself, "My, that looks like fun. I would love to sit on that log."

3. So she tiptoed into the water and approached one end of the floating log. The frogs saw her coming and said, "Hey, what do you think you're doing? Get out of here. Can't you see that this is a frog log, not a cow log?"

Children draw pictures in boxes.

1

2

3

115

4. But when Clarabelle ____________________

Children copy story ending from board.

Children illustrate story ending.

4

Name ____________________ **116**

boy cat girl

The girl had a hat.

The boy had a cat.

116

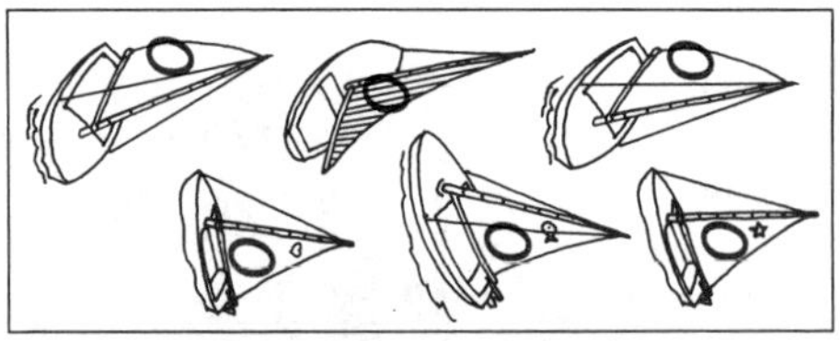

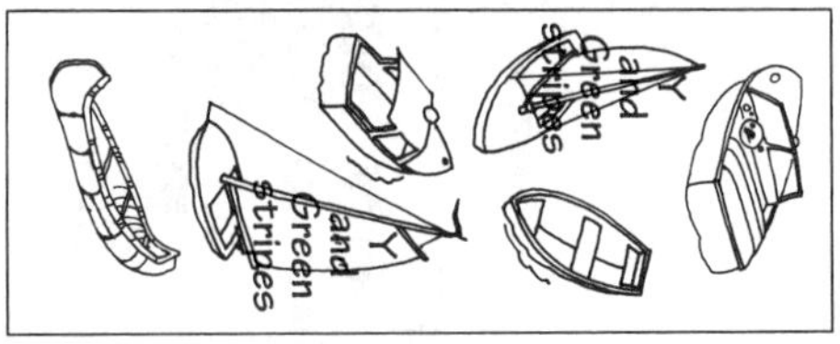

big win push smooth open

1. rough smooth
2. lose win
3. shut open
4. pull push
5. small big

Name ______________________

117

duck barn

The rat was on a barn.

The duck was on a rug.

117

vehicles	colors	plants

truck	vehicles	weed	plants
tree	plants	pink	colors
ship	vehicles	yellow	colors
green	colors	grass	plants
van	vehicles	red	colors

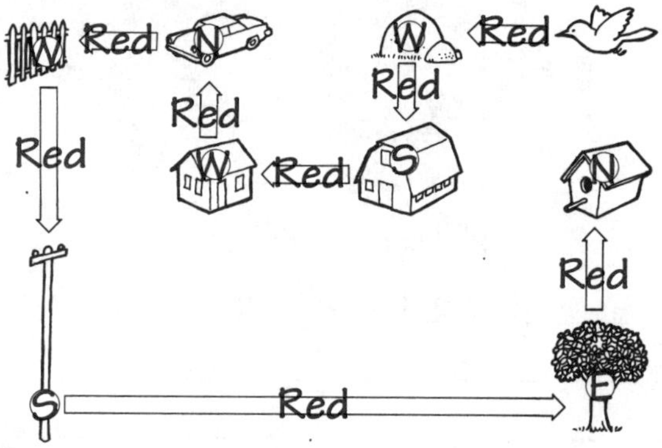

Name ______________________

118

1. Paul
   a. **(true)** false
   b. **(true)** false
   c. true **(false)**
2. Molly
   a. **(true)** false
   b. true **(false)**
   c. **(true)** false
3. Clarabelle
   a. **(true)** false
   b. **(true)** false
   c. true **(false)**
4. Bragging Rat
   a. **(true)** false
   b. true **(false)**
   c. **(true)** false

118

hole mouse

The dog was in a bed.

The mouse was in a hole.

Name _____

| will | stick | turn |

The cat will turn.

The stick will burn.

yellow and red boxes

blue and yellow boxes

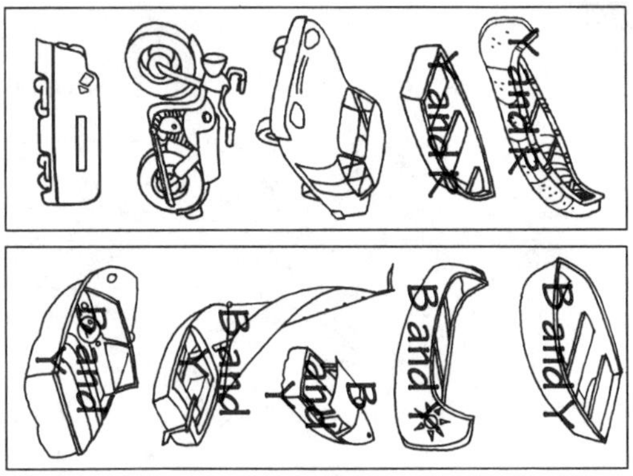

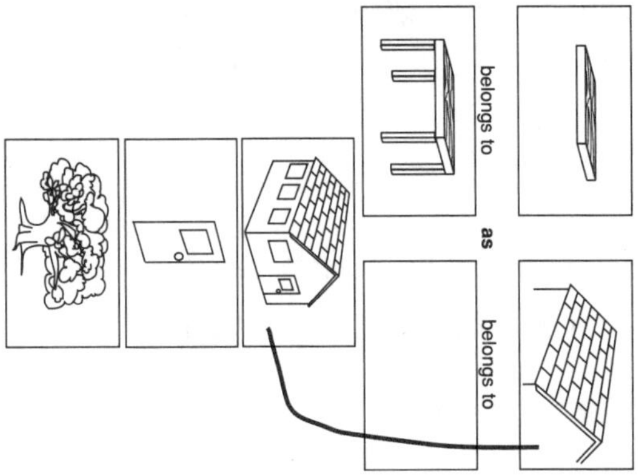

belongs to

as

belongs to

54

Name _____

A B C D E F G H I J K L M N O

C D E F G H I J K L M N O P Q

Clarabelle sat on a little chair.

| Children compose own similar sentences. |

The chair broke.

| Clarabelle | little | chair | broke |

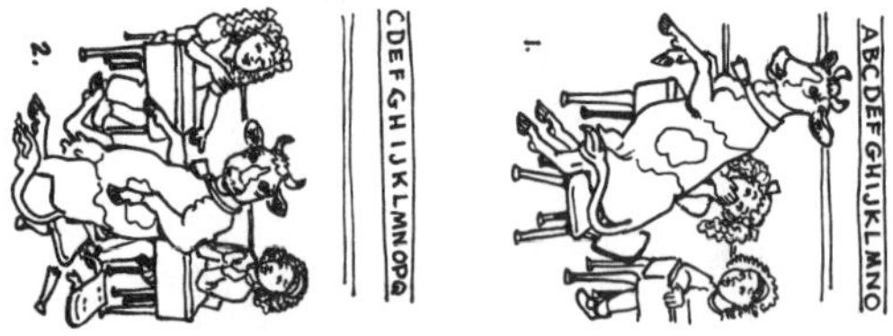

1.

2.

3.

4.

5.

6.

7.

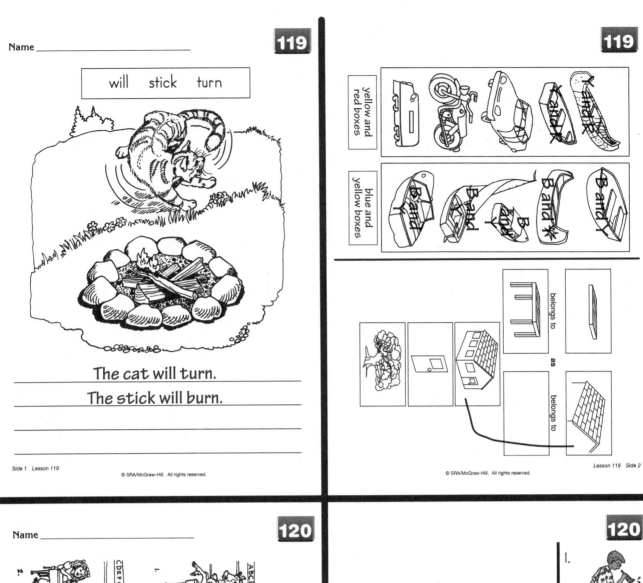

| near | cop |

The fox was near a cop.

The rat was near a mop.

_____

_____

Lesson 121 Side 1

| quiet | shallow | cooked | short |

1. long _____ short _____

2. deep _____ shallow _____

3. loud _____ quiet _____

4. raw _____ cooked _____

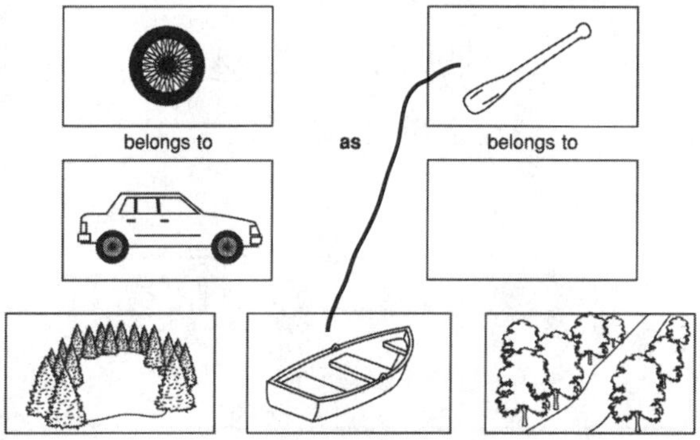

belongs to   as   belongs to

Side 2 Lesson 121

55

| balls | black | boat | white |

The black balls were in a van.

The white balls were in a boat.

_____

_____

Lesson 122 Side 1

---

yellow hats on black birds

red hats on black birds

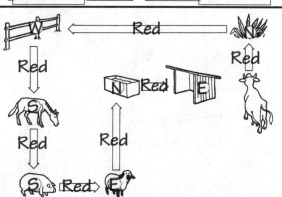

Name ______________________

123

a. kite 4

b. hat 2

c. wrecking yard 3

d. turtle 4

e. pond 1

Side 1 Lesson 123

123

f. honey 5

g. number 1 7

h. bus 6

i. Bleep 9

j. palms 8

Lesson 123 Side 2

56

Name ______________________

124

licked ear cow

The cat licked a hand.

The cow licked an ear.

Side 1 Lesson 124

124

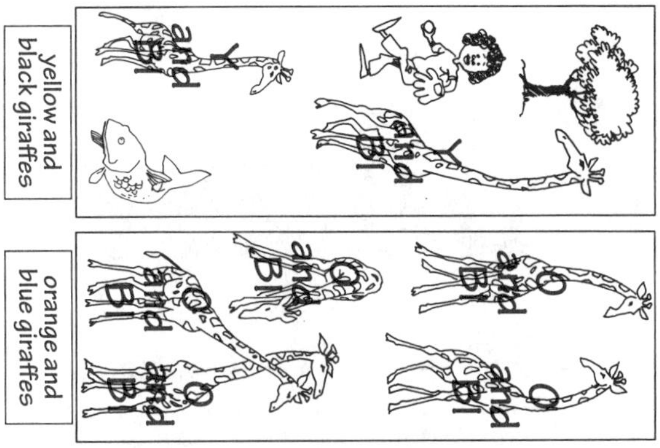

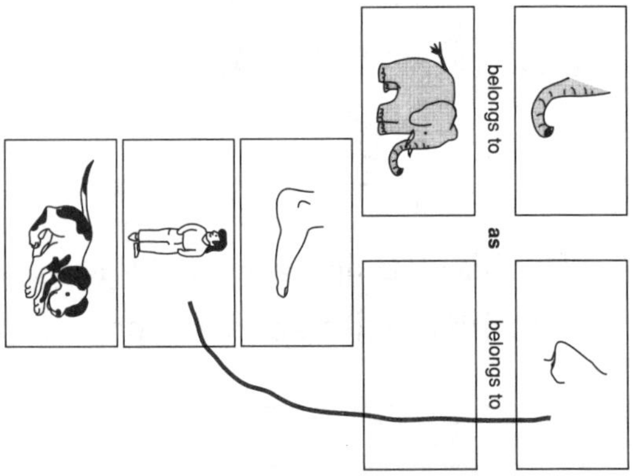

Lesson 124 Side 2

Name _____

125

Sweetie Andrea Honey bit chased

Sweetie chased Andrea.

So Honey bit Sweetie's tail.

Lesson 125 Side 1

125

wide	shiny	pull	short	long

1. tall _____ short

2. push _____ pull

3. narrow _____ wide

4. dull _____ shiny

5. short _____ long

containers	numbers	tools

jar containers

saw tools

ten numbers

cup containers

mop tools

six numbers

bag containers

rake tools

three numbers

nine numbers

Lesson 125 Side 2

126

Name _____

black   white

The toad will go in the white car.

The bird will go in the black car.

_____

Side 1 Lesson 126

126

cry	short	difficult	wide	dark

1. easy _____ difficult

2. laugh _____ cry

3. light _____ dark

4. narrow _____ wide

5. tall _____ short

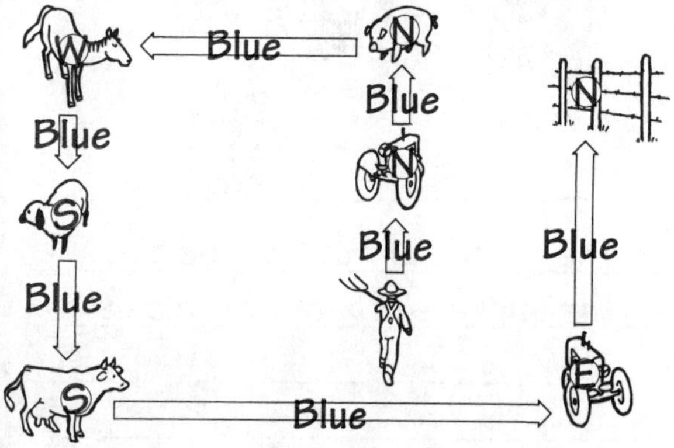

Name ____________________

127

1. Roger had many favorite hats. But his most favorite was a big black hat. One day, he put on that hat and went out for a walk. The day was very hot and Roger started to sweat.

2. Roger didn't want to sweat all over his very favorite hat. So he took off his hat and put it under a bench that was next to a house. Roger planned to finish his walk without his hat, come back to the bench, pick up his black hat and go back home.

3. What Roger didn't know was that the bench was next to Paul's house and that Paul planned to paint that bench pink. Roger also didn't know that when Paul painted things, he plopped paint on things that were nearby.

Children draw pictures in boxes.

1

2

3

127

4. So, while Roger was on his walk, Paul came out and

Children copy story ending from board.

Children illustrate story ending.

4

Name ____________________

128

front	of	back

The goat is in front of the car.

The snake is in back of the car.

128

sad	clean	push	near	dirty

1. dirty clean
2. clean dirty
3. far near
4. happy sad
5. pull push

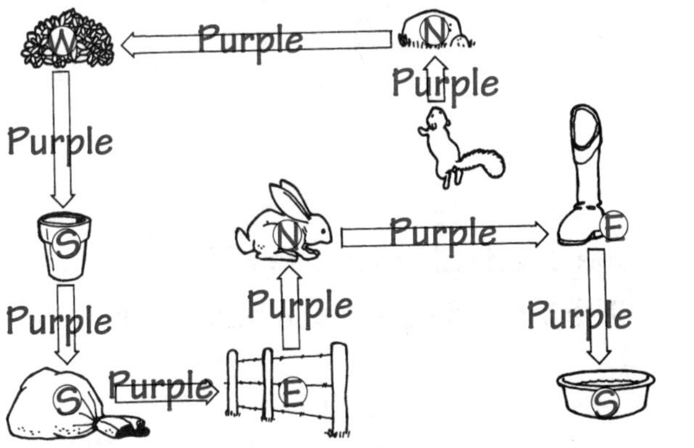

Name ____________________

129

tiger front of
eagle back

The eagle is in front of the tree.

The tiger is in back of the tree.

129

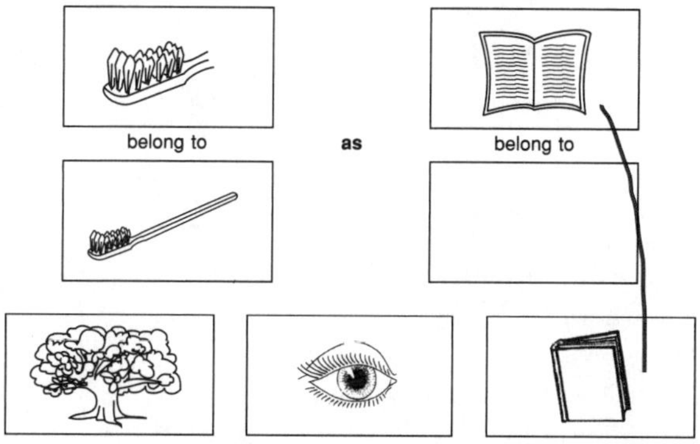

vehicles	animals	clothing

sock	clothing	turtle	animals
boat	vehicles	tractor	vehicles
shark	animals	mole	animals
hat	clothing	dress	clothing
train	vehicles	car	vehicles

Name ____________________

130

☐ Paul

☐ Sweetie

☐ Rolla

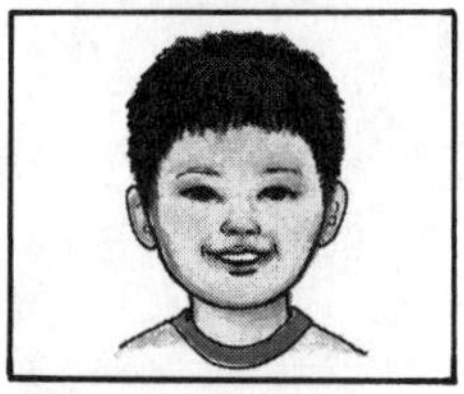

☐ Roger

☐ Honey

☐ Roxie

130

☐ Bleep and Molly

☐ Clarabelle

☐ Bragging Rats

Children check three of the characters in this workbook lesson.